People Power

People Power

Fifty Peacemakers and
Their Communities

MICHAEL TRUE

*For Tim,
with appreciation and
admiration,
Mike
September 4, 2009*

RAWAT PUBLICATIONS

Jaipur • New Delhi • Bangalore • Mumbai • Hyderabad • Guwahati

ISBN 81-316-0087-4
© Author, 2007

*Poems by Denise Levertov reprinted by permission of Denise Levertov
Trust, Paul A. Lacey, Trustee.*

Published by
Prem Rawat for **Rawat Publications**
Satyam Apts, Sector 3, Jawahar Nagar, Jaipur 302 004 (India)
Phone: 0141 265 1748 / 7006 Fax: 0141 265 1748
E-mail: info@rawatbooks.com
Website: www.rawatbooks.com

New Delhi Office
4858/24, Ansari Road, Daryaganj, New Delhi 110 002
Phone: 011 2326 3290

Also at Bangalore, Mumbai, Hyderabad and Guwahati

Typeset by Rawat Computers, Jaipur
Printed at Chaman Enterprises, New Delhi

To Gene Sharp

Contents

Introduction

The title of this collection of portraits, "People Power," associated with the nonviolent overthrow of Marcos in the Philippines in 1986, suggests what nonviolent action is about. It's a method or strategy for resisting injustice and humiliation, for resolving or transforming conflict, and for bringing about social change without killing or harming people.

These men and women, often "ordinary people", have successfully applied these strategies for justice and peace in various parts of the world. Over the past two centuries, they have endeavored to understand a concept and to demonstrate its capabilities for peacemaking in the midst of violence and injustice. Some called it "non-resistance," others, "passive resistance" or "nonviolence"—all inadequate attempts to "name" their efforts to offer a vital, realistic alternative to war-making.

Since 1973, Gene Sharp, the person to whom this book is dedicated, has done more than anyone to clarify the language and methods of nonviolent action and to provide research and scholarship on what works, what doesn't work and why. Indispensable resources by him and his associates at the Albert Einstein Institution, Boston, include *Waging Nonviolent Struggle: 20th Century Practice and 21st Century Potential*. Boston: Porter

Sargent, 2005, and *Protest, Power, and Change: Encyclopedia of Nonviolence From Women's Suffrage to ACT-UP*. New York: Garland Publishing Co., 1995.

This book focuses on men and women who, by their lives and writings, have contributed or continue to contribute to the rich and extensive history of "people power." Each one is representative of people and communities who deserve equal attention—unnamed heroes and heroines who gave their own lives, rather than take the lives of others, in building cultures of peace and justice. I am grateful to them, particularly the late Ammon Hennacy, who first brought many of them to my attention, and to others whose research and scholarship are noted at the end of each portrait. I also appreciate the assistance of Mary Pat True and Carmella Murphy, Assumption College, who helped revise portraits that appeared in slightly different form in my *Justice Seekers, Peace Makers: 32 Portraits in Courage* (1985) and *To Construct Peace: 30 More Justice Seekers, Peacemakers* (1992).

Every day, in every part of the globe, nonviolent activists offer concrete alternatives to violence and injustice by constructing cultures of peace in the face of overwhelming odds. We rightly place our hope for the future on these personifications of love, courage, and wisdom in our midst.

Young Catholic Workers

The origins are positively biblical: a mustard seed fell on rocky soil at Union Square, near 14th Street and Broadway, in New York City. It has grown into a deeply-rooted, sheltering tree—today an arboretum.

In Spokane, Colorado Springs, Davenport, Rock Hill, and Worcester, as well as in Los Angeles, St. Louis, Chicago, Baltimore, and New York, and in the Netherlands and Australia, street people find food, clothing, and shelter in soup kitchens maintained by young Catholic Workers. Since 1933, when its members first distributed 2,500 copies of the Catholic Worker newspaper in Lower Manhattan, the Catholic Worker movement has provided hospitality for hundreds of thousands of men and women whom nobody else cared about.

Initiated by Peter Maurin (1879-1949), an itinerate teacher and worker, and Dorothy Day (1897-1980), a journalist, shortly after their first meeting in December 1932, the movement has drawn three generations of talented workers and organizers, writers and artists, into its network. In the process, it has remained a significant influence on American Catholicism, as well as on the social, intellectual, and literary history of the U.S.

3

By her life and writings, Dorothy Day is surely the most visible and influential figure in the movement. But she regarded Peter Maurin as her teacher; because of them, thousands of "ordinary people" have helped to initiate houses, farms, newspapers, and campaigns for nonviolent social change for over six decades. Some spent a brief period with the Worker—among them Michael Harrington, John Cogley, Ade Bethune, J.F. Powers, William Everson, John Cort, Jim Forest, Charlie King; others have spent much of their lives—Ammon Hennacy, Karl Meyer, Frank Donovan, Rita Corbin, Brendan and Willa Walsh, Tom and Monica Cornell. Workers include scores of priests, nuns, and laity, many of them well-known in various professions and walks of life. Because of their admiration for Dorothy Day, their contributions to the movement, or their writings about her, many others have regarded themselves as "fellow travelers" of the movement. These include Gordon Zahn, Robert Coles, William Miller, not to mention the W.H. Auden, Thomas Merton, and Fritz Eichenberg.

Visiting the hundred or more houses across the U.S., one inevitably meets young men and women, many of them students, for whom the Catholic Worker has been a kind of "agronomic university," as Peter Maurin hoped it would be. There, they learn much about "the whole rotten system," as Dorothy Day used to say, and meet the victims of violence and injustice for the first time. There young people learn how to become "part of the solution" rather than remain "part of the problem." Many go on to extend "the beloved community" through their own efforts, as they live lives of voluntary poverty among the poor or follow a more conventional pattern of marriage, family, and profession. Whatever they choose to do, their lives carry the mark of days, months, or years actively involved with the Catholic Worker, and through them the movement continues to flourish into the third generation.

Daily, across the U.S., young Catholic Workers feed the hungry, house the homeless, set up food pantries and medical treatment centers, comfort the sick, bury the dead, periodically

4

going to trial or into jail for resisting capital punishment, the arms race, and other injustices.

Each day the thriving movement seems, to an outsider, a kind of miracle; some people give their lives for these values; others have their houses closed down for failing to meet a local building code. In June 1991, Matt Devenney of the Community Stewpot, in Jackson, Mississippi, was actually gunned down by a regular patron with a history of mental illness; Devenney, a 33-year-old husband and father, had directed the Stewpot for several years. Other young workers simply burn out, after years of sharing the daily rough and tumble of the inner city's endless stream of "undeserving poor," as Bernard Shaw called them, that line up for soup and hospitality and whatever else is freely offered.

Around these Catholic Worker Houses, other life-giving communities form, some agitating for farm workers' or women's rights, environmental protection or credit unions, land trusts, peace fellowships, draft and war tax resistance. How lucky any community is that harbors a Catholic Worker house, for the unaccounted, often unacknowledged blessings it brings in helping to preserve community in urban settings otherwise rife with violence, hunger, poverty, and neglect.

Each community varies, each a kind of oasis in which these values are made visible and concrete. And after over seven decades, a library of fiction, poetry, plays, artwork, films, and nonfiction tells the story, so that no child growing up and surely no person associated with Christianity should remain ignorant of its powerful example.

Dorothy Day, a born storyteller, understood the power of narrative as the instrument of "spreading the word;" she told the Catholic Worker story over and over again, especially in *The Long Loneliness* (1952), the story of her conversion, and *The Loaves and Fishes* (1963), and continually in her monthly column, "On Pilgrimage." So did Ammon Hennacy in *The Book of Ammon* (1954, 1970) and Robert Ellsberg, in his introduction to *The Selected Writings of Dorothy Day*.

At the end of *The Long Loneliness,* Dorothy Day wrote, "We have all known the long loneliness and we have learned that the only solution is love and that love comes with community. It all happened while we sat there talking, and it is still going on." Fifty years after she wrote that memorable sentence, it's still going on, in evenings of clarification of thought at houses across the U.S., at Ammon Hennacy House in Los Angeles and at the Dorothy Day Soup Kitchen in Rock Hill, South Carolina, in the pages of the *Catholic Worker* and *The Catholic Radical.*

There are many models for the Catholic Worker and many routes to it. Some Houses serve twelve people one meal a week; some serve six hundred people three meals a day. Some Houses take in anyone without a place to sleep. Some distribute free food from a continually replenished pantry, while others house people visiting relatives at state or federal prisons.

Some Workers devote their lives to the movement; others stay for awhile, then move on to other commitments. Scott and Claire Schaeffer-Duffy, for example, who met shortly after they graduated from Holy Cross College and the University of Virginia, Charlottesville, respectively, set up houses for men and women in a rough neighborhood in Washington, D.C. After their marriage, they moved to Worcester, Massachusetts, where they established the House of SS. Francis and Therese, and where they live with their four children and various guests, publish a handsome, informative quarterly, *The Catholic Radical,* and go to trial and to jail for civil disobedience at Raytheon and similar plants that make weapons of mass destruction; at Electric Boat, Groton, Connecticut, which manufactures and launches nuclear submarines; or at Westover, Massachusetts, Airforce Base, from which bombers flew to Vietnam, the Persian Gulf, and Iraq. The Schaeffer-Duffys also teach religious education to children in a local parish, run a summer peace camp for children, and sell bran muffins and wheat bread to raise money for their projects.

At Viva House Catholic Worker, Willa Bickhham and Brendan Walsh live in Baltimore's inner city, where they feed thirty people three times a week and provide hospitality and health care for needy people. On the walls of the soup kitchen and dining room, Willa's silk screens tell part of the story of their commitment to nonviolent social change. The Walshs moved to the city and married several years before they supported the Catonsville Nine (Philip Berrigan, Tom Lewis, Tom and Marjorie Melville, and others) who burned draft files in an effort to end the Vietnam war.

Similarly, Brian Terrell and Betsy Keenan married, after working together at St. Joseph's House in Lower Manhattan and the Catholic Worker Farm in Tivoli, New York. Following seven years at Peter Maurin House, Davenport, Iowa, they homesteaded four acres of land, sell rag rugs and small crafts in Maloy, Iowa, 100 miles southwest of Des Moines.

In Hawaii, on that state's "big island," Jim Albertini and his wife oversee a Catholic Worker farm and retreat center. He too spent time in jail, for "swimming in" to protest nuclear weapons in and around Pearl Harbor. And in Rock Hill, South Carolina, a community of parents and grade school children, with encouragement from David Valtierra, Congregation of the Oratory, initiated a Dorothy Day Soup Kitchen.

Just off Second Avenue, and around the corner from the best Ukrainian restaurant in lower Manhattan, Jane Sammon and Frank Donovan oversee the many activities of the Catholic Worker's "national office." They edit the monthly *Catholic Worker*, still a penny a copy, as it was in the 1930s, with informative articles on the nonviolent movements for social change, with letters from houses and communities around the world, and announcements of Friday Evening "Clarifications of Thought"—poetry readings or urgent messages from young activists and scholars. At the New York houses, as well as at the Marquette University archives in Milwaukee, journalists and historians, young students and seasoned scholars drop by for news and information for anthologies of writings or portraits (like this one) of Catholic Workers, young and old, active or deceased.

Thus do Houses of Hospitality, "agronomic universities," and other Catholic Worker communities continue to flourish, much as Peter Maurin envisioned them decades ago. First he, then Ammon Hennacy, pushed Dorothy Day along a

7

pilgrimage that she followed and chartered for so many others, including the talented, resourceful, and courageous young men and women who carry it on.

By Catholic Workers

By Little and By Little: Selected Writings of Dorothy Day. Ed. Robert Ellsberg, New York: Alfred A. Knopf, 1983.

Cook, Jack. *Rags of Time: A Season in Prison.* Boston: Beacon Press, 1972.

A Revolution of the Heart: Essays on the Catholic Worker. Ed. Patrick G. Coy, Philadelphia: Temple University Press, 1988.

Ellis, Mark H. *A Year at the Catholic Worker.* New York: Paulist Press, 1978.

About Catholic Workers

Coles, Robert, and Jon Erikson. *A Spectacle Unto the World: The Catholic Worker Movement.* New York: Viking Press, 1973.

Miller, William D. *A Harsh and Dreadful Love: Dorothy Day and the Catholic Worker Movement.* New York: Liveright, 1973.

Piehl, Mel. *Breaking Bread: The Catholic Worker and the Origin of Catholic Radicalism in America.* Philadelphia: Temple University Press, 1982.

Stephen Biko (1946-77)
Nelson Mandela (1918-)

You can blow out a candle
But you can't blow out a fire
Once the flame begins to catch
The wind will blow it higher
Oh Biko, Biko, because Biko...
The eyes of the world are
watching now...

He was "quite simply the greatest man I have ever had the privilege to know," according to a writer who met and interviewed many world leaders. Donald Woods wrote that Stephen Biko "had the most impressive array of qualities and abilities in that sphere of life which determines the fates of most people—politics."

For a man who died when he was only thirty and never traveled outside his own country, Stephen Biko had a remarkable following; as the editors of *Christianity and Crisis* said at the time of his death, his face and mind were known across the world. Decades later, he occupies a special place among people struggling for human rights—in history and

9

literature, in film (especially the award-winning *Cry, Freedom*) and song (Peter Gabriel's "Biko," quoted above).

Biko became famous as a leader in the struggle to end apartheid and to build a democratic society in South Africa. In death, he joined thousands of black people who, like him, had been victimized by white settlers since foreign settlements in the mid-17th century. Often torn by tribal conflicts and inter-racial battles, Africans had neither guns nor horses to face the superior technology of white invaders until the end of the 18th century.

Over three centuries, many white people died also in conflicts between white Afrikaners—descendants of early Dutch, German, and Huguenot—and later British-settlers. As the twentieth century began, these two groups fought one another in the Boer War. Shortly afterward, Mohandas Gandhi led an important movement resisting discrimination against Indians, before he returned to his native country and helped to end British rule. Among the recent major figures in South African history are Albert Luthuli, Archbishop Desmond Tutu, and Nelson Mandela, all of whom received the Nobel Prize for Peace. In an historic moment, Mandela was elected president of South Africa in 1994, after spending twenty-seven years in prison, as a member of the African National Congress.

Since 1948, the Nationalist Party had been the party in power, dominated by Afrikaners, who make up 60 percent of the white population in South Africa. In its efforts to perpetuate rule by a white minority, in a country in which 80 percent of the people are black, the Nationalists implemented a number of repressive measures; systematically carried out, these apartheid policies confined blacks to particular regions of the country and denied them basic human rights. Of several major black leaders associated with this terrible period, after the Sharpeville Massacre (1960), which killed 70 Africans, wounded 186 others, and evoked protests from people around the world, Stephen Biko was among the first to die.

It happened in this way. In 1961, in an effort to crush two popular black movements, the Nationalist Party banned Mandela's African Nationalist Congress and Robert Sobukwe's

Rosa Parks   Noam Chomsky

Howard Zinn   Stephen Biko

Pan-Africanist Congress, then imprisoned the two leaders and their chief lieutenants on Robben Island in Table Bay. After a period of some uncertainty, a young Bantu, Stephen Biko, emerged as a vigorous and popular leader. As the first president of the South African Students' Organization (SASO) in the 1960s, he had come to understand that "the most powerful weapon in the hands of the oppressor was the mind of the oppressed." His response to this condition was the founding of the Black Consciousness Movement, which he regarded as "the cultural and political revival of an oppressed people," with the general goal of liberating black people "first from psychological oppression by themselves through inferiority complex and secondly from the physical oppression accruing out of living in a white racist society," as a SASO resolution put it.

Born in King William's Town, South Africa, on December 18, 1946, Bantu Stephen Biko (Bee-kaw) attended primary school there and in Lovedale, a famous missionary school for blacks before a student strike led to its being closed down. After a strong academic performance at Marianhill, a Catholic high school in Natal, Biko spent the years 1966 to 1972 at the University of Natal, with plans initially to study medicine. During that period, however, politics intervened, when his contemporaries responded to the unassuming yet firm leadership that would characterize his life from that point on.

Described as "full of charm, large and easy and gentle and courteous and humorous," Biko was by all accounts a remarkable presence even as a young man, with an impressive command of language, as his speeches and court testimony suggest. "Everyone who met Steve in goodwill experienced a sort of magnetism," Dr. Trudi Thomas wrote. "I attribute it to his triumphant, unassailable normality, a touchstone you were welcome to share."

When officials forced him to leave the university in 1972, Biko was already the acknowledged leader of the South African Students Organization and the Black Community Programs. As a full-time organizer, he publicized the Black Consciousness movement that he had initiated. Within the year, however, he

12

was banned from Durban, where he had been working, and returned to his hometown to work in the same program until he was placed under further restrictions in 1975. Although he traveled extensively after that, he had to do so secretly, protected by an increasing number of followers and admirers, both black militants and white supporters.

For a man who had braved so much, at such terrible risk, the end was swift and brutal. Arrested on September 6, 1977, Stephen Biko was taken by police to a building in Port Elizabeth, Cape Province, where they bound his hands and feet to a grille and interrogated him for twenty-two hours; during that period, he was beaten so fiercely about the head that he fell into a coma and died six days later.

Two weeks later, 20,000 people traveled from all over South Africa to King William's Town to attend Biko's funeral; others were arrested, tear-gassed, and beaten by police in their attempts to join the crowd of mourners. At an inquiry into the causes of his death—in spite of convincing evidence, photographs and testimony to the contrary—the magistrate at the hearing took only one minute to rule that Stephen Biko had died of injuries endured during a scuffle. In a remarkable account of this and other events, Donald Woods, a white journalist, provided transcripts of Biko's trials, including the inquiry after his death; smuggled out of the country, then completed after the author and his family escaped into exile, the book—and a subsequent film based upon it—gave Biko's story to the world.

Prosecuted many times during his short life for minor offenses (a common fate of activists under seige by the white political police), Stephen Biko won the respect even of those who carried out the laws perpetuating apartheid in the courtrooms and jails of his country. Among many testimonies, his eloquent defense of nine young blacks prosecuted by the country's Supreme Court in 1976 is perhaps the best known. There, as on previous occasions, he turned the courtroom into a forum for black grievances against a repressive and racist government, while at the same time defending Black

Consciousness as a constructive rather than a destructive philosophy.

According to many accounts, Biko consistently separated the Nationalist mentality that subjugated him from the individuals caught up in the system. Such behavior reflected the strength and subtlety of his character, evident in many settings, as well as the strong religious influences that echoed in his speeches, interviews, and occasional writings. Not surprisingly, several tributes at the time of his death emphasized his importance not only as a political theorist, but also as a lay theologian.

Although reared an Anglican and educated in church-related schools, Biko saw African Christianity as a colonial inheritance, a product of and symbol of imperial Europe; "the mainline churches were hardly influenced by the black fact," he said. For that reason, he regarded the questioning attitude of black theology in the late 1960s as its most important contribution, challenging "not Christianity itself, but its Western package, in order to discover what the Christian faith means for our continent."

Black theology provided an opportunity "to bring back God" to black people, to the truth and reality of their situation. Black-consciousness-theology was a means for Black Africans to reclaim what was rightfully theirs. In this way, Biko belongs to a special company of martyrs whose leadership contributed to a religious awakening accompanying other recent movements for social change around the world.

Much better known than Biko, of course, Nelson Mandela has played a central role in his county's history for half a century. Born into a noble Xhosa family in Umtata, Transkei, in 1918, he graduated from college and Witwatersrand University, and after 1952 practiced law in Johannesburg. Arrested in 1956 on charges of treason, he was acquitted and released in 1962. Arrested again following a memorable speech in 1964, in which he said he was prepared to die to end white supremacy in South Africa, he was sentenced to life imprisonment.

14   Mandela spent the following twenty-seven years, until 1990, in various prisons, while maintaining his dignity among

his fellow prisoners and his popularity among the wider population. On his release, he reinstituted the African National Congress, and traveled widely in the Middle East, Europe, and North America, where he addressed both the U.S. Congress and the United Nations. Four years later, he was elected president of his country, serving in that role until his retirement, as one of the most admired political figures in modern history.

By Stephen Biko and Nelson Mandela

"Steve Biko Speaks: Our Strategy for Liberation," *Christianity and Crisis*, January 16, 1978, 329-32.

The Challenge of Black Theology in South Africa. Basil Moore, Ed. Atlanta: John Knox Press (1973), 1974.

Mandela, Nelson. *Long Walk to Freedom: The Autobiography of Nelson Mandela.* Boston: Little Brown, 1994.

About Stephen Biko and Nelson Mandela

American Friends Service Committee. *South Africa: Challenge and Hope.* Lyle Tatum, Rev. ed. New York: Hill and Wang, 1987.

Meer, Fatima, *Higher than Hope: The Authorized Biography of Nelson Mandela.* Hamish Hamilton, 1990.

Wilmore, Gayraud S. "Steve Biko, Martyr," *Christianity and Crisis.* October 17, 1977, 239-40.

Woods, Donald. *Biko.* New York: Paddington Press, Ltd., 1978.

Chinese Students

Being sentenced, I will speak my piece,
saying to the world, "I accuse!"
And although you trod a thousand resisters under foot,
I shall be the one-thousand-and-first.

—Bei Dao

Avoiding the line of march so as not to be branded "a foreign instigator," I accompanied the students and faculty each morning in late May 1989, as they left the gates of Nanjing University to walk to Gu Lou Square at the center of the city. The Bell Tower above the square where they gathered for speeches and, eventually, a fast, was immediately recognizable to anyone in China, though not as well-known to the rest of the world as Tiananmen Square, where protests against government corruption originated several weeks before.

Deeply moved by the students' protest, their discipline and intelligence in explaining the nature of their protest to workers and townspeople, I knew—as they knew—the likely consequences of their nonviolent resistance to a repressive State. Yet even party members, including university officials, joined in the protest and publicly supported the students. Days later, groups of young people left Nanjing on "the long march" to Beijing, 700 miles north, to join their contemporaries and former schoolmates. After the June 4 massacre of students in Beijing, shot down by government troops on the edge of Tiananmen Square, however, faculty members and officials in Nanjing sent buses north to pick up the students and bring them back. Shortly afterward, university officials and Jiangsu provincial officials (governing an area the size of New York State, with 60 million people) closed the universities—a wise move to discourage intervention by the army, stationed on the outskirts of the city.

In the history of nonviolent social change, the Chinese students who initiated the campaign for reform in 1989 claim a special place. Their effort, "one of the largest and best organized nonviolent political protest movements the world has ever seen," as Orville Schell wrote, will be a subject for study and reflection by anyone seriously committed to constructing peace and to rebuilding the social order. So it is appropriate that the Albert Einstein Institution at Harvard University and peace research centers are engaged in an on-going study of the movement.

Observing those young people at close range, in Shanghai, Nanjing, and Harbin—before and after the June 4 suppression—I was often reminded of similar movements against corruption and oppression throughout the world, particularly those in the Southern United States during the height of the Civil Rights movement and in New England during resistance to the wars in Southeast Asia and the Persian Gulf.

Throughout China in the spring of 1989, as in the Southern U.S. in the winter of 1960, students gave meaning to democracy each day, taking their message to the wider community through wall posters, demonstrations, and speeches. As with those involved in voter registration in Mississippi and lunch counter sit-ins in North Carolina, young people gave voice to the hopes and grievances of their elders, many of whom had suffered previously under a repressive political system.

Although Nanjing had been the site of demonstrations in **17** April 1989, university students in that "southern capital" (200 miles west of Shanghai, on the Yangtze River) had little formal organization prior to mid-May. During the initial stages of the protests, before being joined by thousands from other universities throughout the city, students, "with their knees knocking" as one observer said, gathered at the Nanjing University gate for the first march to Gu Lou Square.

By mid-May, their contemporaries and close friends in Beijing—calling for an end to nepotism, government corruption, and press censorship—had clearly struck a note that reverberated in the hearts and minds of millions. In giving encouragement and support to students throughout the country, workers and peasants, as well as intellectuals, artists, and teachers, revived a tradition associated with another historic protest seventy years before. In the May 4 Movement, 1919, a previous generation of students had called their elders to account and by their effort had furthered the birth of modern China.

By late May 1989, people in every major city had joined the struggle with demonstrations and hunger strikes. A crowd of 100,000 people poured into the streets of Nanjing, blocking the pedicab carrying my driver, luggage, and me from the train station to the university, as I arrived from Shanghai. Quotations on posters and banners from Chinese poets, ancient and modern, as well as from Lord Acton ("Absolute power corrupts absolutely") and Martin Luther King ("I have a dream...") reflected the students' impatience with the party leadership under Deng Xiaoping and Li Peng.

Like their parents and teachers, students in Nanjing knew well the effects of inflation and wide-scale government corruption that accompanied the previous decade of economic reform. Although some people had profited by a freer market and life generally had improved for many Chinese between 1979 and 1989, people on fixed incomes had to moonlight or to dip into small savings in order to pay the rapidly increasing prices for food and clothing. Public knowledge about party officials getting rich because of their control over the distribution of goods and services had made many people openly cynical about "the old men" ruling the national government.

In earlier student protests, beginning in 1986, student slogans about democratic reform had been rather vague and grandiose. Even the demonstrations in April 1989, after the death of Hu Yaobang, an official popular among university students, were festive rather than political. By May 18, the day of my arrival in Nanjing, the demonstrations focused upon particular grievances, including a party chief's editorial denunciation of the student movement. Perhaps hardly noticed elsewhere in the world, in China, this development suggested a clarification of goals and purposes among young activists and the wider community.

In over 350 cities, as in Beijing, where a young woman, Chai Ling, had assumed leadership of the movement, many journalists working for the government-controlled media supported the students by joining the demonstrations or providing extensive coverage on radio and television—a noteworthy contribution to the nonviolent movement. Student successes in gaining popular support grew, as the young "intellectuals," often resented by workers and townspeople, entered and leafletted factories and workplaces, explaining their campaign to everyone. As did many adults, I admired the students' resourcefulness and restraint and their patriotic spirit. The movement grew.

By late May, faculty, including members of the Communist Party, also signed wall posters and spoke at demonstrations. For a time, the government media transmitted accurate accounts of events at Tiananmen Square and elsewhere, whetting the people's appetite for accurate information and precise details regarding reform. Then, the government imposed martial law; and although wall posters and slogans became increasingly hostile toward Li Peng, the crowds in Nanjing remained purposeful and calm in their requests that the government retract its denunciation of the student movement and initiate reforms. The movement had spread through numerous other cities to Harbin, 700 miles north of Beijing, where I attended an international conference on American literature in early June.

Then, on June 4, came the crackdown, swift and brutal, in **19** the streets of Beijing, with threats of similar reprisals against the students and workers in other major cities. The re-writing of "history" to conform to the party-line began immediately, with government news agencies jumbling dates and scenes of the army's entrance into Beijing. In interviews that appeared rehearsed, "ordinary people" gave their versions of the June 4 massacre and offered flowers and food to "heroic soldiers" who had "defended the nation" against "counter-revolutionary elements," "rascals," and "hoodlums."

Following the killings in Beijing, some people cried out for vengeance against the government, smearing the Chinese character for "blood" across wall posters, drawing caricatures of government officials as Nazis wearing swastikas, particularly after news reached Harbin that four students from the University of Science and Technology had died in Beijing. Such responses were understandable, but in this case, as in most others involving citizens' efforts against the State, the weapons for vengeance, for blood, were all on the government's side.

Faculty everywhere wanted no students walking directly into another senseless slaughter. Then, as now, any direct confrontation with the government seemed not only unwise, but suicidal, though the struggle for freedom of the press and an end to autocratic rule and corruption in high places continued by other means.

Among the many people I spoke with in China, before and after June 4, no one—neither Chinese nor foreigner—anticipated the brutality of the government's response. Gradually, however, people began to understand the historic, then tragic events within the context of recent history. The year before the struggle, in tracing the course of economic and political reforms since Mao's death, Harry Harding had recognized, for example, that "despite the sometimes dramatic cycles in reform since 1978, the most difficult stage in the course of China's second revolution may still lie ahead."

Following the repression, many people outside China wondered how best to support those who had already taken such risks for political reform out of loyalty to their country and concern for its welfare. Returning from China later that fateful summer, I often remembered a Nanjing friend's response when I asked him what a foreigner might do to keep alive the memory of the students in Tiananmen Square and elsewhere. In a late-night conversation, and again before I left for Shanghai and the long flight home, he focused upon this issue: some means of transmitting information by television to the people of China, some means of reaching the millions who rely for news only on official channels with their lies and propaganda.

During the student demonstrations, rumor had it that some soldiers in Beijing with access to international news decided not to fire on their countrymen and women. According to my Chinese friend, similar incidents in India, where people tapped into Western news sources, had strengthened the public to resist oppression there. In China, anyone listening to foreign broadcasts may retain some perspective on events, in the face of the government's re-writing of history; but the return of Hong Kong to Chinese rule may further reduce peoples' access to these alternate sources of information.

"One of the worst aspects of living in brisk, dictatorial China," as Paul Theroux has said, "is that you seldom have an accurate idea of what is really going on." Where 70 percent live on the land, sources of reliable information are severely restricted. Even though students returning from the universities took word of the pro-democracy movement to their homes and communities, for example, they represent a small fraction of the population. And the nonviolent movement, particularly, depends upon broad dissemination of accurate information about issues and events.

Because of its manipulation of the news, the government won a propaganda war and convinced many people that in Beijing the casualties were few. It even succeeded temporarily in re-writing the history of the movement. But too many people tasted the flavor of free speech to forget their appetite for a more open society. Or so it seems to anyone attentive to the costly victories of the students' movement in speaking truth to power.

21

Since 1989, the Chinese have had, once again, to face hard choices and personal sacrifices in order to keep alive the spirit of the movement. Detailed accounts of strategies employed in confrontations with the government, including the army, have already contributed to our knowledge and understanding of nonviolence in that culture. As with Martin Luther King and his associates in the civil rights movement, Chinese students learned quickly as they went along, improvising and keeping alert in the face of overwhelming odds. Finally, in desperation and cynicism, people in power resorted to murder, as they have previously in China and elsewhere.

Someday, nonetheless, a space near Tiananmen Square will undoubtedly be set apart as a memorial to these students and workers—a reminder of their gifts to the people of China and, by extension, to citizens everywhere. "The sacrifice of the students at Tiananmen Square, in all its dignity and power," Christopher Kruegler wrote in the New York *Times*, is rightly compared to that of the people who died at Amritsar in India or in Mississippi and other movements for social justice. In our hearts and memories, those young people deserve a very special place, particularly for anyone committed to nonviolent social change.

By Chinese Students

Li Lu. *Moving the Mountain: My Life in China*. New York: Putnam, 1990.

About Chinese Students

Black, George and Robin Munro, *Black Hands of Beijing: Lives of Defiance in China's Democracy Movement*. New York: John Wiley, 1993.

22 Butterfield, Fox. *China: Alive in the Bitter Sea*, Rev. ed. New York: Random House, 1990.

June Four. A Chronicle of the Chinese Democratic Uprising. Tr. Jin Jiang and Qin Zhou. Fayetteville: University of Arkansas Press, 1991.

Joshua Paulson, "Uprising and Repression in China," in Gene Sharp, *Waging Nonviolent Struggle: 20th Century Practice and 21st Century Potential.* Boston: Porter Sargent Publishers, 2005, pp. 253-69.

Schell, Orville. "China's Spring," *New York Review of Books.* June 29, 1989, 3-4, 6-8.

True, Michael, "The 1989 Democratic Uprising in China: A Nonviolent Perspective," in *An Anthology of Nonviolence: Historical and Contemporary Voices,* Ed. Krishna Mallick and Doris Hunter. Westport, CT: Greenwood Press, 2002.

The Sanctuary Movement &
School of Americas Watch

Across the desert of southwestern Arizona several people walk, having left a Guatemalan or Salvadoran village several days before. It is 1981. Earlier, they traveled by crowded bus or car north into Mexico, then—with the help of guides (called coyotes)—headed toward the United States. Their families and neighbors encouraged them to leave their homeland, after friends and associates were tortured and murdered by uniformed death squads, after young sons from their area had been carried away as conscripts for the military. Those killed had done nothing more than read the Bible or teach catechism, with a nun and priest who had helped them form a cooperative and build a well and community shelter.

Having followed guides through a barbed-wire fence on the American border, then over a mountain range, they are now on their own, with little idea of their exact location. And they wonder, will anyone help once they reach their destination? The coyotes probably abandoned the group for several reasons. They may have thought, first of all, that this mission is doomed; and they want to avoid discovery, fearing they might lose the opportunity of offering their illicit, expensive "services" to other refugees.

Both adults and children in the group must make their way quickly, secretly. Their water supply may not hold out. What they fear most is being arrested as illegal aliens and returned to their country, since returnees are seldom heard of again. (Many are also arrested in Mexico or in the U.S. and held in prison, knowing nothing of their rights.) One thing for sure, they will never sign a form enabling U.S. Immigration and Naturalization Service authorities to send them back home.

Some variation of this story unfolded many times during the early 1980s, along the Mexican-American border from the Rio Grande Valley in Texas, across to Lower California and the Pacific Ocean. Such stories, almost a literary genre, resemble earlier ones involving black families leaving the South prior to the Civil War; Jews escaping Germany and elsewhere in Europe during the 1930s; Tibetans abandoning their homeland after the Chinese invasion and seeking refuge in India during the 1960s, and others escaping repression in this cruel century.

Ironically—and tragically, these Central American refugees fled governments that have enjoyed extensive military and economic aid from the United States; and the death squads who killed their families and neighbors are armed with weapons from, and trained by, experts at military posts in "the land of the free." Although the suffering endured by Central Americans resembles that of the world's refugees, the circumstances that provoked their suffering are peculiar. So are the events that led to the harassment endured by U.S. citizens trying to stop it.

The story of the sanctuary movement, in other words, is twofold, involving (1) landless peasants and some city dwellers facing death in Central America; and (2) "ordinary" middle-class citizens of the U.S. risking jail in order to protect them. The first part of the story, recounted above, has its origins in the structural violence of a system that keeps people illiterate and landless. The second part, discussed below, has its origins in the structural violence of a system in the U.S. that fosters **25** ignorance and irresponsibility.

As their only hope of survival, the refugees escaped the conditions of one system by leaving their native countries. The second group, U.S. citizens of the sanctuary movement, challenged and altered slightly the conditions of the other system, as previous citizens of this country have done, by acts of courage. They resisted unjust laws and risked civil disobedience; more importantly, they built a community of support in order to correct the injustices which they had previously tolerated.

Although the American side of the story began in the Southwest, it gradually involved many areas of the U.S., as people's awareness of the conditions among refugees became known and churches, religious congregations, and households opened their doors, in states as far apart as Minnesota and Maine. As their education—a kind of radicalization—progressed, citizens of the U.S. began to make connections between themselves and their neighbors and the relationship between U.S. foreign policy and the border scene described above. As a result, they reclaimed "a preferential option for the poor," the same one to which the Latin American church had committed itself at Medellin in 1968 after the Second Vatican Council. In a more secular, political manner, U. S. citizens also reminded themselves (and others) of Thomas Jefferson's dictum that "government is for the living."

The initial response in the early 1980s to the Central Americans who showed up along the Southern Arizona border could hardly have been more modest. Local residents, even those who knew something about conditions in Central America, thought these Spanish-speaking refugees were simply Mexicans coming into the state to work. Gradually, a Quaker rancher, Jim Corbett, and clergy who had spoken with Salvadorans in prison learned why so many refugees took dangerous risks to escape their governments.

By 1981, an estimated eighty Salvadorans a week, on their way to the U.S., were deported by the Mexican government. This happened as a result of a "neighborly" agreement with the U.S. government. By June of that year, Jim Corbett had talked with enough refugees to realize that rather than being illegal

26

aliens, they were actually "political refugees, deserving political asylum in the United States," as Miriam Davidson writes in her powerful narrative about Corbett and the sanctuary movement.

Although the details and events reflect the peculiarities of the Reagan/Bush administration and its "war against the poor" in the U.S. and its war against "the threat" of liberation theology, sanctuary members behaved rather as residents of New England once did when they refused to obey the Fugitive Slave Law of 1850 requiring them to return slaves to their slave masters. By yet another underground railway during the Vietnam war, ministers and teachers helped draft resisters or soldiers who were denied conscientious objector status to escape to Canada.

By its Central American policy under Reagan, the United States supported increased repression in Guatemala and El Salvador. Meanwhile, along its Southwestern border, Americans accepted the immigration office's description of the refugees as "just some more Mexican aliens" coming over the border to make money; in reality, they were political refugees with a legitimate claim—according to a United Nations ruling—to political asylum. Fortunately, some "helpers" came to the rescue of the refugees, providing sanctuary in Arizona and beyond. In doing so, they found themselves in conflict with neighbors and parishioners and formed communities of support to protect political refugees not only from some foreign despots, but from representatives of the U.S. government, particularly the Office of Immigration and Naturalization. In 1984, a judge in the Tucson Sanctuary Trial found eleven people guilty of breaking the law; in part because of the trial's visibility and public support for what the defendants had done, they were given suspended sentences. The sanctuary movement grew.

In resisting their government and in their arguments before the court in the 1984 trial, members said they acted within a tradition as old as the U.S. itself. As Jim Corbett argued, "From the Declaration of Independence to the trials at Nuremberg, our country has recognized that good citizenship   27 requires that we disobey laws or officials whenever they mandate the violation of human rights. A government that commits crimes against humanity forfeits its claim to legitimacy."

In building a community of support for the refugees and in reawakening their churches, the movement has helped to bring a version of the Latin American base communities to the U.S. and to give it indigenous roots. Vicki Kemper, commenting on the 1984 trial, suggested how this community building is accomplished, often by church workers who don't necessarily know one another. The diverse group in Tucson, "with different theologies, ministries, and politics," came together and stayed together "because of their common commitment to Central American refugees, a commitment so strong that it overshadowed all their differences."

The sanctuary movement has helped those involved, as it did Jim Corbett, to discover "the church in its broadest sense" as a community "ready to respond to violations of human rights." By embodying what he calls "faith as trust" rather than "faith as belief," the movement helped to inform an even larger effort, since 1989, to close the School of Americas at Ft Benning, Georgia, where the U.S. trains military personnel, sometimes in torture, from throughout Latin America.

Initiated by Roy Bourgeois, a Maryknoll priest, SOA Watch has grown in size and significance since then, as one of the most extensive and sophisticated legislative and direct action movements in modern U.S. history. Each November ten to twenty thousand people of all ages gather at the gate of Ft. Benning, calling for the closure of the so-called "School of Assassins," which, under this pressure, changed its name to the Western Hemisphere Institute for Security Cooperation. (A response to the name change by the late Congressman Joseph Moakley of Massachusetts: "That's like pouring perfume on a nuclear dump.") In recent years, many participants at the November protest have risked jail or gone to prison for several months as a result of crossing the boundary of the military post.

28   The story of Roy Bourgeois commitment to closing the School of Americas and the educational, direct action, and

legislative movement that he has succeeded in building is a powerful one, not easily conveyed in a brief description. Born in Louisiana, he is a veteran of the Vietnam war, where he met a priest who headed an orphanage for children victimized by the war, and subsequently studied for the priesthood with the Missionary Society of the United States (Maryknoll). After spending seven years as a priest in Latin American, among the poor, he was forced out of Bolivia in 1977. Returning to the U.S., he became increasingly involved in efforts to end American military aid to Central America, and coordinated an award-winning film, *Gods of Medal* (1983), on that topic. In 1993, he protested the training of Salvadoran soldiers by the U.S. at Ft. Benning, by broadcasting the final sermon of Oscar Romero, Archbishop of San Salvador, who was murdered four years earlier by soldiers trained in the U.S.

Bourgeois' increasing involvement, including arrests and public protests, evoked strong criticism from a variety of communities, including concerns among his religious superiors and even death threats, when he rented an apartment on near the main gate of Ft. Benning. Through it all, he remained faithful to his vocation as a priest, and increasingly effective in his lectures and national organizing to close the School of Americas. Meanwhile, the legislative campaign to cut the funding for "School of Assassins" gathered the support from Congressman Joseph Kennedy and Congressman James McGovern, both of Massachusetts. At one point, they even succeeded in passing legislation reducing funding, only to have the vote rescinded shortly afterward.

Gaining access to the names of graduates, many of them well-known human rights abusers, with assistance from the United Nations Truth Commission, SOA Watch has also won the hearts and minds of thousands of people. Among recent victories are agreements with the governments of Venezuela, Argentina, and Uruguay to stop sending military personnel from those countries to train at Ft. Benning. Although as Bourgeois has said, "It's hard to hold on to joy and hope over the long haul," he appears not to have faltered in the long, costly, and demanding effort to remain faithful to the people of Latin America "in their struggle for justice."

By Members of the Sanctuary Movement and SOA Watch

Corbett, Jim. *The Sanctuary Church*. Philadelphia: Pendle Hill, 1986.

Hodge, James and Linda Cooper, *Disturbing the Peace: The Story of Father Roy Bourgeois and the Movement to Close the School of the Americas*. Maryknoll, NY: Orbis Books, 2004.

Interviews: John Fife, Peggy Hutchison, Philip Willis Conger, Darlene Nicgorski, Jim Corbett, *Sojourners*. XV, 7 (July 1986), 20-30.

About the Sanctuary Movement and SOA Watch

Davidson, Miriam. *Convictions of the Heart: Jim Corbett and the Sanctuary Movement*. Tucson: University of Arizona Press, 1988.

Golden, Renny, and Michael McConnell. *Sanctuary: The New Underground Railroad*. Maryknoll, N.Y.: Orbis Books, 1986.

Nelson-Pallmeyer, Jack. *School of Assassins: Guns, Breed, and Globalization*. Maryknoll, NY: Orbis Books, 2003.

Sanctuary: A Resource Guide for Understanding and Participating in the Central American Refugees' Struggle. Ed. Gary MacEoin. San Francisco: Harper & Row, 1985.

Vandana Shiva (1952-)

Since the death of Gandhi in 1948, the nonviolent tradition in India maintains his legacy in a number of ways, through governmental organizations, such as the Gandhi Peace Foundation, International Center for Gandhian Studies and Research, at the Raj Ghat, and the Gandhi Smriti and Darshan Smriti, at Birla House, Delhi. Gandhi's legacy remains most vital, in numerous non-governmental organizations, in the lives and campaigns of activists over the past half-century. They include the Sarvodaya movement, led by Vinoba Bhave (1895-1982) and J.P. Narayan (1902-79), and more recent initiatives such as the Shanti Sena (Peace Army) and, in 1981, Peace Brigades International, co-founded by Narayan Desai and, in Sri Lanka, the Sarvoda Shramadan movement headed by A.T. Aryaratne. Acknowledging the achievement of Gandhi and the National Movement, Arundhati Roy, a nonviolent activist and critic of the Narmada dam project, argues that circumstances "are entirely changed now," with "The Hindu Nuclear Bomb," as legacy of that National Movement.

"Women's understanding of the social systems in which they live has been profound and often pathbreaking," as Elise

Boulding wrote in *Cultures of Peace* (2000). Such women would include Roy, as well as Dr. Wangari Maathai, a Nobel Peace Laureate from Kenya, and Dr. Vandana Shiva, a physicist and eco-feminist, also from India. Born in Dehra Dun in 1952, the daughter of a forester, Vandana Shiva grew up in the Himalayan forests, was educated in India and abroad, and completed her doctorate in the philosophy of science in 1978. During graduate study in Canada, she was shocked to learn that the World Bank had provided huge subsidies to finance the conversion of food-growing land to timber-growing land in various parts of the world. Returning home, she taught herself agro-science and biotechnology and established her reputation as a thoughtful, persistent critic of Western-style agriculture and development. An activist and scholar, she initiated the Research Foundation for Science, Technology and Ecology, a modest enterprise "started in my mother's cow shed," in 1990.

Brought up by a mother who was a staunch Gandhian, Shiva wore *khadi* (handspun clothing) as a child, and maintains very political links with Gandhi, "because I do not believe there is any other politics available to us in...a period of a totalitarianism linked with the market. There is no other way you can do politics and create freedom for people without the kinds of instruments he revived. Civil disobedience is a way to create permanent democracy, perennial democracy, a direct democracy."

In criticizing the Tropical Forestry Action Plan, Vandana Shiva was deeply influenced by the Chipko "embrace-the trees" Movement, in which Alaknanda Valley peasants and farmers in the Himalayan foothills, stopped lumber companies from clear-cutting mountain slopes. Logging and destruction there led to a dramatic increase in floods and landslides that endangered water and fuel sources. Crying, "You will have to chop us up before you chop this tree," ordinary women initiated a resistance movement that spread from village to village, dramatizing the connection between ecology and community development. As Chandi Prasad Bhatt, Chipko's founder, argued, "If we are not in a good relationship with the

32

environment, the environment will be destroyed, and we will lose our ground. But if you halt the erosion of humankind, humankind will halt the erosion of the soil." Vandana Shiva was drawn to a movement-in-progress "long after it had been given its articulation by the women," without external leadership. She named its source "stri shakti" (women's power), "that amazing power of being able to stand with total courage in the face of total power and not be afraid."

Relying on Indian spiritual and nonviolent traditions, Dr. Shiva exposed the bias of modern science and politics on environmental issues in her area of the world, in a movement to conserve native seeds and to prevent the domination and seizure of genetic processes by multi-national corporations. She challenged RiceTec Corporation, for example, in its attempt to patent Basmati rice "which women farmers in my valley have been growing for centuries," she said, as well as other corporations who claim property rights as a reward for their investment in food research. Navadanya (nine seeds), a movement Shiva initiated, advocates for biodiversity conservation and farmers' rights, and identifies forces driving water scarcity and threatening its future supply.

Shiva maintains that agribusiness is subsidized by the poorest of families and children, with Monsanto, for example, "making money by coercing and literally forcing people to pay for what was free," such as water. That company patented genetically engineered seed that didn't germinate on harvest, so that farmers remained at the mercy of the company for renewal of their crops. She quoted the head of the Coca-Cola Company saying that its biggest market in India "comes from the fact that there is no drinking water left. People will have to buy Coca-Cola."

In a significant crisis in the contemporary world, "governments and political processes have been hijacked by the corporate world," with immediate access to and heavily influenced votes in the U.S. Congress and the Indian Parliament. Shiva calls this phenomenon "the inverted state, where the state is no longer accountable to the people. The state only

33

serves the interests of corporations." Free trade policies associated with the North American Free Trade Agreement (NAFTA) and the General Agreement on Tariffs and Trade (GATT), she argues, are the modern counterpart to the Papal Bull, an edict in 1493 that legitimized European conquest of the world. She remains very skeptical, also, of the forces of globalization, whose theme is "find markets where you can." Expanding the market in this manner leads to the privatization of everything "seeds, medicinal plants, water, land. All the land reforms of India are being undone by trade liberalization," which Shiva calls "anti-reform reform."

Sometimes regarded as a person who offers critiques rather than alternatives to globalization, through analysis combining eco-feminism and sustainable development, Shiva has successfully dramatized relationships among a wide range of concerns related to justice and peace. The Right Livelihood Award, which she received in 1993, and the Earth Day International Award of the United Nations, 2000, recognized her success in bringing complex issues of environmentalism, feminism, and community action to a large audience.

By Vandana Shiva

Biopolitics: A Feminist and Ecological Reader on Biotechnology. Atlantic Highlands, NJ: Zed Books, 1995.

Ecofeminism, with Maria Mies. London: Fernwood/Zed, 1993.

Interview by David Barsamian. *Progressive,* September 1997, pp. 26-29.

Interview by Nic Paget-Clarke (Earth Summit, Johannesburg, South Africa), *Motion Magazine,* March 6, 2003.

Staying Alive: Women, Ecology and Development. London: Zed, 1989.

Stolen Harvest: The Hijacking of the Global Food Supply. Cambridge, MA: South End Press, 2000.

Water Wars: Privatization, Pollution, and Profit. Cambridge, MA: South End Press, 2002.

About Gandhian Movements in India

Roy, Arundhati, *The Cost of Living*. New York: Modern Library, 1999.

Shepard, Mark, *Gandhi Today: The Story of Mahatma Gandhi's Successors*. Cabin John, MD: Seven Locks Press, 1986.

Greenham Common Women

"As a woman, I have no country...as a woman, my country is the whole world."

—Virgina Woolf

The initial media response to the Greenham Common Women—"the harridans of Greenham Common"—was predictable. Others expressed their hatred of women activists in similar clichés.

Remembering these and similar reports from the 1980s makes one wonder if historians may eventually regard the decade as the worst, politically, in our time. Was there ever a succession of presidential administrations in the U.S., for example, when mean-spiritedness, deception, and greed were so blatant? Has public opinion ever shown such contempt for the poor, the down-and-out, the vulnerable? Were the rich and powerful ever so crass, so unfeeling? As billions of dollars were appropriated and spent on weapons of war—in direct proportion to the increase in homeless, hungry people—policies leading to these conditions went practically unchallenged by otherwise decent citizens. Even powerful congressional leaders regarded opposing the Reagan administration as political suicide, when the global consequences of its policies were overt and covert wars in the Middle East, Latin America, Southeast Asia, the Caribbean.

At the same time, a small band of resisters advocated alternative policies and initiated programs of public moral education. In the U.S., it included the Clamshell Alliance, the Atlantic and Pacific Life Communities. Among these and similar faithful witnesses, no one was more persistent, faithful, and imaginative than the Greenham Common Women in England. In defying the deadly duo, Reagan/Thatcher, these women initiated and maintained a decade-long campaign to halt the proliferation of nuclear missiles at an American base, "USAF Greenham Common," just south of London. "We are not on trial. You are," Katrina Howse told the court on November 17, 1982, in Newbury, Berkshire. The power the court uses to support nuclear weapons, she continued "supports binding women's voices, binding our minds and bodies in prison so our voices cannot be heard .... But we cannot be silenced. And I cannot be bound over." In addressing the magistrates, Katrina Howse joined thousands of women who had been camping on Greenham Common for over a year, protesting the largest cache of nuclear missiles in Europe.

A December 1979 decision by the North Atlantic Treaty Organization (NATO) to station 464 land-based U.S. cruise and Pershing II missiles in Europe had prompted the women's persistent daily resistance to nuclear arms on English soil. The decision to put a fourth of the weapons at Greenham Common, the women said, had been taken "over our heads and without our knowledge" and over the heads of most elected Members of Parliament. In an initial action, August 27, 1981, women, children, and men marched from Cardiff, Wales, 125 miles to the "USAF/RAF Greenham Common," near Newbury, southwest of London, to protest that decision. Arriving there, and after being denied a national debate on the issues, they set up a peace camp which eventually inspired similar projects against nuclear missiles throughout Europe.

In December 1982, a month after Katrina Howse's court appearance, 30,000 women circled the nine-mile perimeter

37

fence and sealed off the air base. Like many other women before and since, they endured fines and jail sentences for civil disobedience after repeated attempts by local authorities to evict them by harassment and intimidation. Having previously ignored Greenham Common Women and the dangers and issues surrounding the presence of deadly weapons in their midst, the whole country took notice in 1982, and a national debate ensued. Directly and indirectly, that led to later protests against the nuclear missiles involving hundreds of thousands of people in major cities throughout Europe and over a million people in New York City and, subsequently, to East/West negotiations.

At Greenham Common, as in previous episodes in the history of nonviolence, individual women reclaimed a pacifist tradition initiated by earlier feminists, and brought to life values implicit in women's resistance to war from the 18th century to the present. That tradition had its origins in the Female Auxiliary Peace Societies of the 1820s; Emily Hobhouse and her efforts to draw attention to the suffering of women and children in the Boer War; activists and writers contributing to it included the Austrian Nobel Peace Laureate Bertha von Suttner and the American essayist Charlotte Perkins Gilman.

The connections that Greenham Common Women made—in building "a movement of their own"—between feminism and pacifism, gender and war were ones that Virginia Woolf also had made in *Three Guineas* (1936). Responding to several men who had asked women about how to prevent war, "with the sound of the guns in our ears," Woolf answered:

> We can best help to prevent war not by repeating your words and following your methods but by finding new words and creating new methods. We can best help you to prevent war not by joining your society but by remaining outside your society but in co-operation with its aim. That aim is the same for us both. It is to assert "the rights of all—all men and women—to respect in their persons the great principles of Justice and Equality and Liberty.

Greenham Common Women lived out these ideals in keeping a round-the-clock protest which included cultural events, meetings, and discussions at the site and a wider network of individuals and groups who supported them: the Campaign for Nuclear Disarmament, initiated by Bertrand Russell and chaired at that time by E. P. Thompson; church and union associations, which provided donations supporting the movement; and others who wrote and brought encouragement from countries around the world.

Over the decade, those who carried out this remarkable witness took the values associated with their lives and concerns as "ordinary" women and applied them to the public issues that had been taken out of their hands. In meetings and organizing manuals, which quote from their journals, they brought new insights to essential questions about their own and the world's fate. Among the records of their deliberations and reflections, two having to do with the implications of their own dreams and their experience with the press are particularly interesting.

Generalizing about what women at the camp learned about themselves and nuclear war, participants concluded that the most disturbing aspect is the way dreams "related to the very threat of destruction" hung over their lives and the future.

> The effects of nuclear weapons lie in our heads, as well as in radioactive fallout. The damage that is being done now to people's vision of the future and their faith in future generations is incalculable.

Elsewhere, in commenting on "the highly selective filter of information" through which journalists and editors present issues, they describe conditions that keep the general public ignorant on major political issues:

> As outside observers, [reporters] usually have little information or understanding about how an action is organized or what those involved feel about it. They never admit this limitation even if they are aware of it.

In speaking to the media, women who took risks to get essential information across seldom speak "directly to the audience but through screens, which vary somewhat from editor to editor. Something of what is said gets through—more or less coherently," but it is muddled up or mixed with other, often "louder" voices: press releases from offices of the prime minister or president or others with a stake in the political status quo.

These and similar insights accompanied the women's sustained effort "to construct peace" at Greenham Common, and their history is a useful model. As "About Political Action in Which Each Individual Acts from the Heart," Denise Levertov's poem, says, "When people act in this manner, as these women's actions dramatized, "great energy flows from solitude,/and great power from communion."

By Greenham Common Women

Cook, Alice, and Gwyn Kirk. *Greenham Women Everywhere: Dreams, Ideals and Actions from the Women's Peace Movement.* Boston: South End Press, 1983.

About Greenham Common Women

Fairbairns, Zoe, and James Cameron. *Peace Moves: Nuclear Protest in the 1980s.* London: Chatto and Windus, 1984.

Liddington, Jill. *The Road to Greenham Common: Feminism and Anti-Militarism in Britain Since 1820.* Syracuse: Syracuse University Press, 1992.

Reweaving the Web of Life: Feminism and Nonviolence. Ed. Pam McAllister, Philadelphia: New Society Publishers, 1982.

Virginia Woolf and War: Fiction, Reality, and Myth. Mark Hussey. Syracuse University Press, 1991.

Atlantic and Pacific Life Communities & The Plowshares

Their newspaper combined the wit of a comic strip and the moral clarity of Thoreau's "Civil Disobedience." Its regular feature, "Dear Gandhi: Now What?"—letters and responses in the manner of "Dear Abby"—gave members of the Ground Zero Center for Nonviolent Action, in Washington state, "a way of laughing at ourselves and our ridiculous efforts to learn simple things":

Dear Gandhi,

As a chaplain in the U.S. Navy, I would like your advice on how to preach on Jesus' teaching, "Love your enemies," to the crew members of a Trident submarine.

Sincerely,

Preacher at Sea

Dear Preacher at Sea,

Give each of them a conscientious objector discharge application; then fill one out yourself.

Gandhi

To a reader inquiring about his preference in a presidential election, "Gandhi" offered this advice:

> If he were to run, I would vote for Winston Churchill. Winston is remembered well by the people of your country, and he has now given up cigars, war, and imperialism. Perhaps you can find a candidate there who has done the same.

The Ground Zero Center began as a project of the Pacific Life Community, "a small intentional community committed to resisting the coming of Trident [nuclear submarines] to the Pacific Northwest." As with similar resistance groups across the country, it originated in a simple, courageous act—in this case, Robert Aldridge's resignation from his job as a Lockheed missile designer in 1975 in protest against the building of nuclear weapons systems.

Two years later Jim and Shelley Douglass, creators of "Dear Gandhi," and seven others purchased land next to a Trident base in Bangor, Washington, and committed themselves to a long-term presence on navy-dominated land near Strategic Weapons Facility Pacific (SWFPAC), a nuclear weapons storage center. Fifteen miles across Puget Sound from Seattle, hidden from public view in a heavily wooded area, SWFPAC was circled by high-intensity and double security fences and "patrolled 24 hours a day by Marines armed with dumdum bullets and authorized to use 'deadly force.' "

The Ground Zero community "wanted to experiment with Gandhi's idea that the enemy has a piece of the truth, and with the religious teaching of love for the enemy. We wanted to walk

42

the fine line between hating the sin and loving the sinner, recognizing that we, too, were complicit in violence and thus also sinners," the Douglasses said. Their witness led to various projects, occasionally to jail, and to other people forming networks to resist the deployment of nuclear submarines and weapons.

What began in the Seattle area extended south and east along various routes that carried deadly weapons systems to the rest of the world by land and sea. In 1982, a Peace Blockade, for example, placed forty people in fifteen small boats and two 50-foot sailboats in the path of the USS Ohio, the first Trident submarine, as it entered the Bangor, Washington, naval base. Shortly afterward, the Agape Community grew up along train routes carrying hundreds of warheads and missile motors from the Pantex Plant in Amarillo, Texas, north and west to Utah and Washington, to be assembled in Bangor.

Over a fifteen-year period—and at present—members of the Pacific Life Community have endured arrest and jail for their persistent effort to halt the shipment of deadly weapons. A particularly dramatic incident in its history occurred in 1987, when Brian Willson, a Vietnam veteran from up-state New York, suffered harsh consequences for "making peace." As he lay across the tracks at Concord, California, Naval Weapons Station, a 250,000 pound locomotive carrying arms going to Central America crashed into him. The naval train crew ran over him, rather than remove him from danger. Surviving and eventually walking again, with the help of new prosthetic legs, Willson wrote, ironically, that he enjoyed "more 'standing' as a peace wager" after the accident than before:

> The experience of standing up to the death train and wondering what my survival means has left me with a metaphysical and spiritual consciousness beyond my capacity to put in words. I feel more liberated than ever to share the gift of life .... I am more committed than ever to wage unconditional peace with the empowering force of nonviolence.

On the East Coast, during the same period, the Atlantic Life Community, a similar network of spiritually-based 43 resistance communities, initiated nonviolent actions for disarmament at the Pentagon, the White House, and various nuclear weapons research centers. With Jonah House, Baltimore, as a focal point, the community now extends south to Florida and north to Maine, and includes artists, teachers, psychiatrists, carpenters, clergy, grandmothers, students.

In 1980, several members of the Atlantic Life Community carried out the first Plowshares action, symbolically disarming MX missiles by hammering their nose cones at the General Electric facility in King of Prussia, Pennsylvania. The subsequent trial (later the subject of a film, with Martin Sheen) involved eight defendants: Philip Berrigan, Daniel Berrigan, S.J., Carl Kabat, O.M.I., John Schuchardt, Dean Hammer, Elmer Maas, Anne Montgomery, R.C.S.J., and Molly Rush. The group's name had been suggested by these lines from the Old Testament prophet, Isaiah:

And they shall beat their swords into plowshares,
and their spears into pruning hooks;
nation shall not lift up sword against nation
neither shall they learn war any more.

By 2006, eighty Plowshares groups, unfurling banners on warships and pouring blood on planes armed with other "peacekeepers," had entered various weapons facilities along the East Coast, from Maine to Florida, throughout the Midwest and Southwest, in England, Ireland, Scotland, Germany, and Australia. On Easter Sunday, 1991, at 3:45 A.M., for example, five Aegis Plowshares-Kathy Boylan, Tom Lewis, Barry Roth, Philip Berrigan, and Daniel Sicken-climbed onto the *U.S.S. Gettysburg*, harbored at Bath, Maine, hammered on missile launchers, poured blood, and unfurled banners across the gun mounts. They also posted an indictment charging President Bush and other military chiefs with violations of religious, domestic, and international law in deploying weapons of mass destruction, such as the Tomahawk missiles. Then, for an hour, the Aegis Plowshares tried to find the personnel who were supposed to guard the lethal weapon. Similarly, in April 2002, three Dominican nuns, Sisters Carol Gilbert, Jackie Hudson, and Ardeth Platte, symbolically disarmed a nuclear missile silo in Colorado. In exposing the dangers of possessing such weapons, accessible to anyone looking for them, the Plowshares have repeatedly pointed to a major liability of the nuclear game: our vulnerability before weapons that adventurers peddle for a fast buck, at everyone else's expense around the world.

Plowshares actions result in arrests and sometimes long imprisonment for those who took the risks of disarmament; they also led to extensive public education about the arms race. Periodicals such as *Year One*, books, and documentary films provide the background information and tell the remarkable stories of people going to prison, of courtroom victories and losses, and of a faith sustained by study, work, prayer. At their trials, scholars, clergy, and public figures such as Howard Zinn, Dr. Robert Jay Lifton, Richard Falk, and Ramsey Clark testify as expert witnesses on the American tradition of civil disobedience in the public interest, from the Boston Tea Party through the Civil Rights movement. In time, Fred A. Wilcox, an historian of the movement, wrote, "our grandchildren and great-grandchildren will study Plowshares activists as we now do Harriet Tubman, Sojourner Truth, Martin Luther King, Jr., and Mahatma Gandhi," who were also loved and hated during their lifetimes. In some cases, public support led to charges being dropped against Plowshares, when the defense argues for acquittal on grounds of international law, which regards these weapons of mass destruction as illegal.

Moving testimonies by Plowshares; defendants justifying their actions are a particularly impressive part of this history. The principal justification, in legal terms, emphasizes "the necessity" of the actions for the protection of future generations and the environment. Yet in acting on behalf of all of us, the Plowshares recognize, as Paul Kabat, O.M.I., a defendant in the February 1985 trial, did, that their chances for "success" in stopping the arms race are slim. Responding to a frequently asked question about the effectiveness of his actions, he said:

> In spite of my fantasies I do not expect my act or my resulting years in prison to have any cosmic effect on history, just as I am aware that the quiet deaths of many

45

children in Fourth World situations around the world do not make any real difference to us Americans or to the political and economic leaders of our nation. Millions of children phase out silently and are buried in obscurity. So also, the Silo Pruning Hooks will not be much noted as time and events go by.

One might say of Father Kabat, as of other resisters, what Garry Wills once said of the Jonah House Community: "These are people who simply will not be defeated—who see the world in the bleakest terms, yet sustain most preposterous hope." Commenting on one of its favorite sayings—"The truth will make you odd," by Flannery O'Connor, Wills added, "the truth has not made enough of us odd enough to question the terrible assumptions of our age."

The Atlantic and Pacific Life Communities and the Plowshares, by contrast, not only question the terrible assumptions of the war-making state; they offer radically different assumptions, new beginnings, as strategies for nonviolent social change. As with earlier movements for justice and peace, they build around them what Robert Bly called "small communities of the saved."

By Atlantic and Pacific Life Communities and Plowshares

Berrigan, Philip, and Elizabeth McAlister. *The Time's Discipline: The Beatitudes and Nuclear Resistance.* Baltimore: Fortkamp Publishing Co., 1989.

Douglass, James. "A Nonviolent Activist," and Molly Rush, "A Grandmother and Activist," in *Peace-makers: Christian Voices from the New Abolitionist Movement.* San Francisco: Harper & Row, 1983.

Douglass, Jim and Shelley. *Dear Gandhi: Now What?: Letters from Ground Zero.* Philadelphia: New Society Publishers, 1988.

Swords Into Plowshares: Nonviolent Direct Action for Disarmament. Ed. Arthur J. Laffin and Anne Montgomery. New York: Harper & Row, 1987.

Wilcox, Fred A. *Uncommon Martyrs: The Plowshares Movement and the Catholic Left.* Reading, Mass.: Allison-Wesley, 1991.

About Atlantic and Pacific Life Communities and Plowshares

Wills, Garry. "Inside the Whale." New York *Times,* April 1989.

Peacework: 20 Years of Nonviolent Social Change. Ed. Pat Farren, Baltimore: Fortkamp Publishing Co., 1991.

Martin Luther King, Jr. (1929-68)

Thinking back over his relatively brief public life, one is sometimes astonished to remember that the Civil Rights movement had been in progress for some time before Martin Luther King, Jr., emerged as the principal spokesperson, among a host of equally remarkable men and women.

Yet by background and training, Martin Luther King, Jr. was especially well prepared to make the most of that nonviolent revolution which, in transforming the South, provided a training ground, a school, a university-without-walls for nonviolent activists. Just as the Wobblies, socialists, and anarchists in the decade before the First World War educated labor organizers and reformers for the radical 30s, so the new abolitionists of the Civil Rights movement taught a later generation about nonviolent resistance and agitation for change.

Looking over the names of leaders in the movement to end the Vietnam war and the campaign against the nuclear arms race, as well as in later campaigns for peace and social justice, one can point to many who went South during the 1960s, on Freedom Rides, in voter registration campaigns or the March on Selma. Philip Berrigan, for example, taught in a black school in New Orleans before he burned draft files in Maryland; Abby

Hoffman ran a "Snick" (Student Nonviolent Coordinating Committee) shop, selling crafts from Mississippi before he initiated his "revolution for the hell of it" on the Lower East Side in Manhattan; Howard Zinn and Staughton Lynd taught in a black women's college in Atlanta before Zinn joined Resist in Boston and Lynd became a labor lawyer in Youngstown, Ohio. Similarly, Rosa Parks disobeyed an Alabama law against blacks and Fannie Lou Hamer challenged traditional roles of women in Mississippi before Betty Friedan and Gloria Steinem initiated the feminist movement.

"The son, the grandson, and the great-grandson of preachers," as he tactfully reminded Alabama clergymen addressed in "Letter from Birmingham Jail," Martin Luther King, Jr., was born on January 15, 1929, in Atlanta, Georgia. Educated at Morehouse College there and Crozer Theological Seminary in Pennsylvania, he was ordained a Baptist minister in his father's church at 18. In 1955, he completed a doctorate in systematic theology at Boston University. That December, he called a citywide boycott of segregated buses in Montgomery, Alabama, where he had been serving as pastor of a church for over a year. From then until his death in Memphis in 1968, he coordinated and inspired nonviolent movement for social change focusing on the rights of working people, especially blacks, and resistance to the American war in Southeast Asia.

King's power is evident, not only in his extraordinary courage, but also in his skills as a speaker and writer. His essays, for example, lose little of their effect even years after the events that prompted them have been forgotten. "The Negro Revolution" (1963), characteristic in style and language, makes its point through stories from his own life and those of his associates: "Some years ago," King begins,

> I sat in a Harlem department store, surrounded by hundreds of people. I was autographing copies of Stride Toward Freedom, my book about the Montgomery bus boycott of 1955-56. As I signed my name to a page, I felt something sharp plunge forcefully into my chest. I had been stabbed with a letter opener, struck home by a

49

woman who would later be judged insane. Rushed by ambulance to Harlem Hospital, I lay in a bed for hours while preparations were made to remove the keen-edged knife from my body. Days later, when I was well enough to talk with Dr. Aubrey Maynard, the chief of surgeons who performed the delicate, dangerous operation, I learned the reason for the long delay that preceded surgery. He told me that the razor tip of the instrument had been touching my aorta and that my whole chest had to be opened to extract it. "If you had sneezed during all those hours of waiting," Maynard said, "your aorta would have been punctured and you would have drowned in your own blood." In the summer of 1963, the knife of violence was just that close to the nation's aorta.

Although King's name and achievement are known to many people, the deeper implications of his life, as with those of many peacemakers, are often trivialized or forgotten. This is particularly true of his deep, persistent commitment to nonviolence. Fortunately, however, in *Stride Toward Freedom* (1958), he gives an account of his spiritual odyssey, beginning with his reading of Thoreau in college, and moving on to his reading of Marx, Gandhi, and Reinbold Niebuhr, and hearing A. J. Muste in the seminary.

Although he sided with Gandhi, he had to come to terms with Niebuhr's critique of pacifism. In the intellectual struggle that ensued, King noticed that Niebuhr "interpreted pacifism as a sort of passive resistance to evil expressing naive trust in the power of love. But this was a serious distortion," King concluded.

My study of Gandhi convinced me that true pacifism is not non-resistance to evil, but nonviolent resistance to evil. Between the two positions, there is a world of difference. Gandhi resisted evil with as much vigor and power as the violent resister, but he resisted with love instead of hate. True pacifism is not unrealistic submission to evil power, as Niebuhr contends. It is rather a courageous confrontation of evil by the power of love. . .

Martin Luther King, Jr.   Philip Berrigan

Muriel Rukeyser   Cesar Chavez

Just how fully King took this principle to heart is indicated not only by his rejection of violence in the struggle for black equality, but also in his resistance to militarism and the Vietnam war. The piece of writing for which he is best remembered is a classic essay, equal in power and eloquence to the Declaration of Independence and Thoreau's "Civil Disobedience." "Letter from Birmingham Jail" (1963), addressed to eight Protestant, Catholic, and Jewish clergymen who called King's leadership "unwise and untimely," gives the historical, religious, and political justifications for his actions and helped thereby to win a nation to his cause. Reprinted in newsletters, newspapers, pamphlets, and hooks, it became the Common Sense of the second American revolution. Equally important was his historic address at Riverside Church in New York City, April 4, 1967, "A Time to Break the Silence" attacking the Johnson administration's war policy in Vietnam.

In bringing together the principles of 19th century American abolitionists and non-resisters—Garrison, Thoreau, Ballou and the practical teachings of Tolstoy and Gandhi, King gave the tradition of nonviolence a new and solid grounding in the American experience. In any nonviolent campaign, he says near the beginning of "Letter from Birmingham Jail," there are four basic steps: "(1) collection of the facts to determine whether injustices are alive; (2) negotiation; (3) self-purification; and (4) direct action." Then King shows how he and his associates met each of those conditions in Birmingham, and concludes with this argument for the justice of the black liberation movement:

> Before the pilgrims landed at Plymouth, we were here. Before the pen of Jefferson etched the majestic words of the Declaration of Independence across the pages of history, we were here. For more than two centuries our forbearers labored in this country without wages; they made cotton king; they built the homes of their masters while suffering gross injustice and shameful humiliation—yet out of a bottomless vitality they continued to thrive and develop. If the inexpressible cruelties of slavery could not stop us, the opposition we now face will surely

fail. We will win our freedom because the sacred heritage of our nation and the eternal will of God are embodied in our echoing demands.

Careful study of the last three years of his life deserves particularly study and appreciation. After Civil Right Law was passed in 1965, he initiated a campaign on behalf of poor people, black and white, and then an international effort to end the nuclear arms race.

By Martin Luther King, Jr.

A Testament of Hope: The Essential Writings of Martin Luther King, Jr. Ed. James Melvin Washington. New York: Harper and Row, 1986.

About Martin Luther King, JR.

Branch, Taylor. *At Canaan's Edge: American in the King Years 1965-68.* New York: Simon and Schuster, 2006.

—, *Parting the Waters: American in the King Years 1954-63.* New York: Simon and Schuster, 1988.

Lewis, David L., *King: A Critical Biography.* New York: Praeger, 1970, 1978.

Martin Luther King, Jr.: A Documentary: Montgomery to Memphis. Ed. Flip Schulke. New York: W.W. Norton Co., 1976.

Oates. Stephen B. *Let the Trumpet Sound: The Life of Martin Luther King, Jr.* New York: Harper and Row, 1982.

Noam Chomsky (1928-)

Was Emily Dickinson speaking to critics of U.S. foreign policy (during the Cold, Korean, Vietnam, Persian Gulf, and Iraq wars), when she wrote,

> 'Tis the Majority
> In this, as All, prevail-
> Assent-and you are sane-
> Demur-you're straightway dangerous-
> And handled with a chain-

Hearing Noam Chomsky ridiculed for criticizing C.I.A. interventions and the government's disregard for human rights at home and abroad, I was reminded of Dickinson's warning. Since 2003, however, the general public is less tolerant of government wrong-doing; and information formerly confined to Chomsky's books, columns, and speeches has appeared even in the New York *Times* and on popular news programs.

Until recently, the response to Chomsky's political writings by government "experts" and academic theorists unwilling to look beyond platitudes had been predictably fierce. And commentators in the mass media who seldom imagined or offered political choices beyond (a) and (b) have ignored Chomsky's persistent consideration of (c), (d), (e), (f), and (g). What his critics could not imagine or consider was, to them, "outrageous" (as Gore Vidal, whose insights are similarly dismissed, once put it).

Born in Philadelphia, December 7, 1928, Noam Avram Chomsky is the son of Elsie Simonofsky and William Chomsky, a Hebrew scholar and teacher who immigrated to the U.S. from Russia in 1913. Educated in private and public schools, Noam Chomsky was a junior fellow at Harvard University and, in 1955, completed a Ph.D. degree at the University of Pennsylvania. Since then, he has taught at the Massachusetts Institute of Technology, where he holds a chair in modern languages and linguistics, and for brief periods at other universities in the U.S. and abroad. Married and the father of three children, he has been honored by scholarly societies and universities in this country and abroad, and inevitably draws large crowds in speaking about the foreign policy of his own and other governments. The London *Times*, in referring to him as one of the "makers of the twentieth century," reflects the opinion of contemporary historians regarding his interests and influence.

Chomsky has said that his anarcho-socialist politics were formed by "the radical Jewish community in New York"; those political enthusiasms, in turn, led him to the study of linguistics. As a young man, he took a particular interest in Jewish culture and traditions, and considered moving to Israel. Since 1965, however, he has become one of the principal critics of the American-Israeli alliance, finding the Jewish state no more reliable than other nation-states in its handling of domestic and foreign affairs.

Although clear about options and opportunities available to us for escaping economic and political disaster, Chomsky remains pessimistic about any chance of our choosing them. "What is lacking, primarily, is imagination and will," he has said. A major task involves our confronting a political system "designed to induce passivity, to make it appear that what happens in the world is beyond our control." While hoping that we might overcome perceptions about being powerless in the

face of "some current Great Satan," or other "grand and impersonal forces," he doubts that we will.

A man with a healthy anarchist skepticism toward the
state and a strong stomach for bad news, Noam Chomsky has
undoubtedly saved many lives by "exposing the bastards"
responsible for injustice in their dirty little corners of the world,
in his dogged, informative investigative research on American
foreign policy. Persistent, he has taken risks in order to remain
unrelentingly intellectual and rational in an age and culture
that is highly anti-intellectual and irrational. When the
military- industrial-university complex reigned supreme in the
1980s, he shouted, "The emperor has no clothes!" until that
nakedness became apparent to others who eventually joined
Chomsky in a public chorus. Throughout the "long sleep" that
accompanied the Cold War, he has acted, spoken, and written
with what Francis Hope calls "a proud defensive
independence," retaining a writer's hatred of obfuscation and
resisting the platitudes of contemporary thought.

Long regarded as an important social critic, Chomsky took
his place among the most influential linguists in the world with
the publication of a "pale blue book" called *Syntax Structures*
(1957). Using a mathematical model, he constructed a system of
generative grammar, a kind of "universal" grammar of
languages. Throughout, he has emphasized the difference
between "surface structures," applying to sounds and words in
our sentences, and "deep structures," having to do with how
we derive meaning from them. His sense of a linguistic order
among a multiplicity of languages is reflected in theories that
have influenced not only the way languages are now taught,
but also the way we define ourselves as human, as Daniel
Yergan once said.

Since the early, highly technical treatises on linguistics, he
has also written less technical essays exploring the implications
of studying language for disciplines such as psychology and
philosophy. His speculative and personal Whidden Lectures,
published in *Reflections on Language* (1976), for example, talk
about language as "a mirror of mind," as "a product of human
intelligence created anew in each individual by operations that

lie far beyond the reach of will or consciousness." In suggesting similarities between the growth of language and the development of a bodily organ, Chomsky considers new ways of thinking about thinking and of understanding interactions among language, mind, and other mental organs. In this sense, his impulse to challenge preconceptions about language, which brought him first to public attention, resembles the impulse that led him, later, to challenge preconceptions about political and international affairs in his extraordinarily ambitious, prodigiously documented critiques.

American Power and the New Mandarins (1969), his first book on that topic, introduced a theme that reappears throughout his later writings and numerous speeches, to huge audiences around the world. In that early book, he called bureaucrats and scholars trained by and often housed by the universities "the new mandarins," that is an elite—perhaps even an aristocracy—that tolerates and defends the right of the United States to dominate the globe. Quoting Randolph Bourne, the American literary radical who excoriated American intellectuals for their uncritical endorsement of America's entering World War I, Chomsky took contemporary intellectuals to task for their complicity with the State and their refusal to "speak truth to power."

In a shelf of books, Chomsky's political journalism and social criticism document that charge, with further examples and extensive footnotes. Their common theme is provided by George Orwell's comment, quoted at the beginning of *The Political Economy of Human Rights*: "The nationalist not only does not disapprove of atrocities committed by his own side, but he has a remarkable capacity for not even hearing about them."

Citing extensive statistics and examples in that two-volume study, Chomsky and Edward S. Herman describe the consequences of irresponsible and immoral behavior by leaders and their gullible, sometimes willfully ignorant followers. Discussing relations between the United States and the Third World, the authors focus on domestic institutions, **57** including the mechanisms of propaganda, that cushion any criticism of U.S. policy. Actively supporting that policy are: (1) international businesses that "stifle unions and contain reformist threats" that might interfere with their exercise of power; (2) bankers and industrialists who welcome a new fascist order that suppresses dissidents, priests, labor leaders, peasant organizers. Such people serve as functionaries "playing their assigned roles in a system that has worked according to choice and plan."

Anyone choosing Noam Chomsky's way of taking on the military/industrial/university complex has heavy work cut out for him or her. After the death of Paul Goodman, who joined him in initiating a national organization challenging illegitimate authority, RESIST, Chomsky inherited the mantle of the-critic-that-others-love-most-to-misrepresent. This happened during a "popular" war when Chomsky called U.S. intervention in the Persian Gulf and ultimately in the war on Iraq, a "protection racket for the rich folk"; in a characteristic "transition" Saddam Hussein went from being a "friend," during the Iran-Iraq war, to being "Hitler," as had many previous dictators (Marcos, Noriega) once allied with the U.S. "They're all fine as long as they're our thugs."

In the thick of battle, on the platform or the op-ed page, Chomsky is often remarkably restrained, even discrete—yet persistent, unrelenting. In subsequent writings, he continues to expose the deceit that enables callous or thoughtless leaders to impose their will on vulnerable people.

By Noam Chomsky

American Power and the New Mandarins. New York: Random House, 1969.

The Chomsky Reader. Ed. James Peck. New York: Pantheon, 1987.

Language and Problems of Knowledge: The Managua Lectures. Cambridge, Mass.: M.I.T Press, 1988.

Necessary Illusions: Thought Control in a Democratic Society. Boston: South End Press, 1989.

The Political Economy of Human Rights: The Washington Connection and Third World Fascism, Vol. 1; and *After the Cataclysm: Postwar Indochina and the Construction of Imperial Ideology. Vol. II.,* With Edward Harman. Boston: South End Press, 1979.

Rogue States: The Rule of Force in World Affairs. Boston: South End Press, 2000.

About Noam Chomsky

Leiber, Justin. *Noam Chomsky: A Philosophic Overview.* Boston: Twayne Publishers, 1975.

Lyons, John. *Noam Chomsky.* New York: Viking, 1970.

Thinkers of the Twentieth Century. Gale Publishing Co., 1983.

Cesar Chavez (1927-93)
Dolores Huerta (1930-)

The Scene: 1000 workers demonstrate legally against Vice President George Bush in front of the St. Francis Hotel, San Francisco, in August 1988. Earlier, presidential candidate Bush appeared on television with California's Republican governor eating grapes, ridiculing Cesar Chavez, farm workers, and a grape boycott. Dolores Huerta, vice-president of the United Farm Workers (UFW), responded by saying, "Mr. Bush's statement demonstrates again that he is wealthy and comfortable and insensitive to the struggles of working people in our country. It also reveals his ignorance of the pesticide threat to our environment and our people."

Minutes after she handed out this statement, policemen wielding three-foot batons plunged into the crowd of farm workers and beat Dolores Huerta, five-feet-two-inches tall and weighing 110 pounds, and Howard Wallace, a fellow organizer, in what he later called "a harrowing, terrifying experience." Fortunately for their adversaries, all farm workers had made an absolute commitment to nonviolence years ago. "Nonviolence is a total commitment," Huerta once said. "This is where women are particularly important, because they are preservers."

Following the beating, Huerta ended up in the hospital with a ruptured spleen and fractured ribs. "No one realized how serious her injuries were at first," said Richard Chavez, husband of the middle-aged mother of eleven and grand-mother of ten. Within weeks after her release from the hospital, Huerta traveled the country again, in an organizing effort to stop farm owners from using dangerous pesticides in fields worked by union members.

The sacrifice of Huerta and other farm workers— including Nan Freeman, Nagi Daifallah, and Rufino Contgreras, all of whom died in *la causa*—dramatizes the high cost of their commitment to nonviolence; it helps to explain, also, why the movement has inspired workers all over the world in their struggles for decent wages and working condi-tions, health care, and personal dignity.

Born in Dawson, New Mexico, in 1930, the daughter of farmworker parents, Dolores Huerta moved to California as a young woman. As with Cesar Chavez, her early years as an organizer began with the Community Service Organization, which used the methods of Saul Alinsky, a well-known community organizer in the Chicago area. Alinsky once summarized his principles in a brief manifesto: "No decisions by outside elites; no demagoguery, bombast, or empty threats; rather a long series of small meetings in private homes, gradually joining in a larger structure." (Gandhi had used similar methods when he returned to India in 1915 after the successful campaign in South Africa; so did the leaders of religious reform in Latin America as they formed base commu-nities in the early 1960s.)

Through Fred Ross, her boss in the Community Service Organization, Huerta met Cesar Chavez. In 1962, impressed by the "quiet and unassuming" Chavez, she left C.S.O. to help build the farm worker's union, becoming its first vice-president in 1965. She has remained in that post ever since, serving as a chief negotiator, lobbyist, spokesperson, and strategist. Moving 61 from place to place, Huerta spent less than two months in any location. Characteristic assignments included tours during national boycotts of the United Farm Workers when she traveled throughout New England and spoke as a homilist at a Mass and about nonviolence during conferences of the New England Catholic Peace Fellowship at Mont Marie, Sisters of St. Joseph, Holyoke, Massachusetts, in 1975, and Mount Holyoke College, in 1990, respectively.

In discussing the origins of the United Farm Workers, historians point to similarities between the UFW and other important campaigns for justice in American history. Leadership of effective movements for social change "need not arise from the persons most likely to benefit from it," wrote Joan London and Henry Anderson. Primary leadership for abolishing slavery, for example, "did not and could not come from slaves"; nor did children initiate the movement to abolish child labor. There is a "fine justice," nonetheless, in the way leadership for the United Farm Workers was assumed by people who were themselves the aggrieved ones. Huerta, Cesar Chavez, and other Chicanos (Mexican-Americans) worked in the fields as they organized, lived as farm workers live, and suffered the risks of their difficult lives. Even now, after long experience and an occasional victory, the leaders all look and sound and talk, not as managers or "experts," but as farm workers do.

Cesar Estrada Chavez, like his famous co-worker, is the child of farm-worker parents. Born March 31, 1927, near Yuma, Arizona, in the North Gila Valley, he lived for several years on a farm homesteaded by his grandfather, a refugee from the Mexican revolution. Then came the Depression, "the invisible scar." After losing his farm to a local banker in 1938, Cesar's father was forced to move from place to place, while he, his wife, and children worked as itinerate farmers picking vegetables and fruits in Arizona and California.

During this period, which he described so eloquently to Studs Terkel later, Chavez endured many of the humiliations that make up the life of an itinerant worker's child. He remembered one occasion in particular when his parents drove with the six children through Indio, California, and stopped at a small, road-side restaurant, its window-sign reading "White Trade Only." Chavez's father, who read English without quite understanding the meaning, walked in with "a pot he had, to get some coffee for my mother."

> He asked us not to come in, but we followed him anyway. And this young waitress said, We don't serve Mexicans here. Get out of here.' I was there, and I saw it and heard it. She paid no more attention. I'm sure for the rest of her life she never thought of it again. But every time we thought of it, it hurt us. So we got back in the car and we had a difficult time trying—in fact, we never got the coffee.

During those years, Chavez and his brothers attended, by their own count, thirty-seven elementary schools. "We never got a transfer. Friday, we didn't tell the teacher or anything. We'd just go home....

> I remember one teacher—I wondered why she was asking so many questions. (In those days anybody asked questions, you became suspicious. Either a cop or a social worker.) She was a young teacher, and she just wanted to know why we were behind. One day she drove into the camp. That was quite an event, because we never had a teacher come over. Never. So it was, you know, a very meaningful day for us.... This I remember.... This is the truth, you know. History.

During the Second World War, Chavez enlisted in the navy and spent two years on a destroyer escort in the Pacific theater. Following the war, he returned to San Jose, California, where he had worked earlier, and married Helen Favila. They settled in San Jose "on the wrong side of the tracks" with his in-laws, and worked in the fields. "We figured later that the whole family was making twenty-three cents an hour." In the off season, he took odd jobs; in 1949 the first of their eight children was born.

In the 1950s, Cesar Chavez met a priest who taught him about the social encyclicals of the Catholic church, beginning with Leo XIII's *Rerum Novarum* (1891)—on the rights of

63

workers. In 1962, after ten years with Fred Ross and the Community Service Organization, Chavez left San Jose for Delano, California, to organize the National Farm Workers Association (NFWA), with Dolores Huerta. Both with young—and sizable—families, they took great risks, without any financial assistance from outsiders. In 1963, for example, Chavez turned down a well-paying administrative job with the Peace Corps in South America.

In time, more people, including Catholic clergy and young professionals, came forward to help in organizing and providing services for the farm workers. Through a series of events, in what came to be called "the Delano movement," workers initiated a successful rent strike. In this and a later strike against Schenley Industries, Inc., they began to claim their right to organize, a right not extended to itinerate workers by earlier federal legislation. Some members worked as full-time volunteers, receiving room, board, basic expenses, and $5 a week spending money. Others give a couple of evenings a week or a full day to organize meetings, to circulate petitions, to stand in picket lines at local supermarkets, or to perform basic tasks essential to carrying on a workers' campaign. By 1965, farm workers began to get help from the larger unions, including Longshoremen and Teamsters, who had ignored or actively resisted them earlier.

Since the death of Cesar Chavez, Huerta and her associates, and thousands of people from every background—students, journalists, nuns, doctors, clergymen, lawyers, secretaries—sustain the movement. Others have left to take up political careers or to follow other vocations.

Chavez once argued that a national campaign will succeed if only ten or eleven percent of the people support it. Changing the world, in other words, requires the assistance (or resistance) not of every single person, but of a conscientious, committed minority. The United Farm Workers, as with civil rights and similar movements around the world, requires, also, a disciplined, faithful leadership. Chavez, who died in 1993, often **64** fasted for long periods, as he did for 36 days just prior to the incident involving Huerta in San Francisco. "The fast is the heartfelt prayer for purification and strengthening for all of us," Chavez said afterward, "an act of penance for those of us in moral authority." All the while, adversaries, including agri-businesses linked to national or international corporations have enormous power on their side.

For all these reasons, efforts on behalf of the workers are on-going, even as the union enjoys occasional major and minor victories along the way. Through it all, United Farm Workers have reason to celebrate their success in maintaining the dignity of various minorities and assisting other workers in claiming theirs. In recent decades, they have maintained a persistent campaign to ban the use of harmful chemicals by corporations that cause serious illnesses and death for field workers.

By Dolores Huerta and Cesar Chavez

"Acceptance Speech by Cesar Chavez Upon Receipt of Gandhi Peace Award, 11 May 1989," Promoting Enduring Peace, P.O. Box 5103, Woodmont, Connecticut 06460.

Hard Times: An Oral History of the Great Depression. Ed., Studs Terkel, New York: Random House, 1970, 1986.

About Dolores Huerta and Cesar Chavez

Hope, Marjori and James Young. *The Struggle for Humanity: Agents of Nonviolent Change in a Violent World.* Maryknoll, N.Y.: Orbis Books, 1977.

London, Joan, and Henry Anderson. *So Shall Ye Reap: The Story of Cesar Chavez and the Farm Workers' Movement.* New York: Thomas Y. Crowell, 1970.

Mathiessen, Peter, *Sal Si Puedes.* New York: Random House, 1970.

Denise Levertov (1923-97)

In "Making Peace," a voice cries out from the dark, saying that poets must give us peace "to oust the intense, familiar imagination of disaster." Responding to that challenge, the principal speaker in the poem answers,

> But peace, like a poem,
> is not there ahead of itself...
> can't be known except
> in the words of its making,
> grammar of justice,
> syntax of mutual aid.

Building a new social order and making a new language are parallel activities, calling for a restructuring of life and idiom:

> a line of peace might appear
> if we restructured the sentence our lives are making,
> revoked its reaffirmation of profit and power,
> questioned our need, allowed
> long pauses...

In life, as in art, Levertov's poem suggests, the time has come for a revaluation of values. On that condition rests our hope for appropriate language, to sustain us, and for a new social order.

Some years before Levertov wrote "Making Peace," hundreds of distinguished American artists had endeavored, individually and collectively, to "make peace" by supporting the anti-war effort. From its initiation in 1965 by Robert Bly and David Ray, *Poets Against the War in Vietnam* sponsored benefit readings and public forums on campuses and in communities and helped to clarify the moral and political issues associated with U.S. intervention. In June, the same year, Robert Lowell, perhaps the most "public" poet of his generation, turned down President Lyndon Johnson's invitation to a White House Festival of the Arts because of Johnson's war. In a carefully written, even courteous letter, Lowell warned that the administration's policy toward Vietnam put the U.S. "in danger of imperceptibly becoming an explosive and suddenly chauvinistic nation." Other writers, including Stanley Kunitz, Bernard Malamud, Mary McCarthy, and Dwight McDonald, supporting Lowell's decision, expressed "dismay at recent American foreign policy decisions."

Other artists described the agony and suffering inflicted by military forces on both sides, and in *Armies of the Night. The Novel as History, the History as Novel* (1968), Norman Mailer gave a moving, autobiographical narrative about the 1967 March on the Pentagon, which brought a hundred thousand people to a major demonstration in Washington. Well-known poets took political risks in addressing moral questions associated with American policy by writing poems of remarkable artistic skill and integrity and by committing acts of civil disobedience against the war and the draft. In 1968, at a ceremony in New York City, as Vice President Hubert Humphrey looked on, Robert Bly gave the $1,000 check accompanying his National Book Award for *The Light Around the Body* (1967) to a young draft resister, Michael Kempton. Similarly,

DENISE LEVERTOV

Muriel Rukeyser endured arrest in anti-draft demonstrations, and Allen Ginsberg, echoing Henry David Thoreau's "Civil Disobedience," encouraged citizens to refuse to pay taxes supporting war.

Among the many lyric poems that took the Vietnam war as a theme, Robert Bly's "Asian Peace Offers Rejected Without Publication" conveys the despair that many Americans felt as the troop shipments increased from fifty thousand to two-hundred-fifty thousand to five-hundred thousand American soldiers and as negotiations for a cease-fire failed again and again. As Bly suggests in this eloquent poem, neither presidents nor advisers had any intention of ending the war:

> These suggestions by Asians are not taken seriously.
> We know Rusk smiles as he passes them to someone.
> Men like Rusk are not men only
> They are bombs waiting to be loaded in a darkened hangar.
> Rusk's assistants eat hurriedly,
> Talking of Teilhard de Chardin,
> Longing to get back to their offices
> So they can cling to the underside of the steel wings
> shuddering faintly in the high altitudes.

Other poems of similar skill that took the war as their theme include Robert Bly's long poem, *The Teeth Mother Naked at Last* (1970); and lyrics such as David Ignatow's "All Quiet— Written at the start of one of our bombing pauses over North Vietnam"; Muriel Rukeyser's "Poem," beginning "I lived in the first century of world war"; Allen Ginsberg's "Wichita Vortex Sutra"; Levertov's remarkable collection *The Sorrow Dance* (1967); and other poems based upon actual experience in Vietnam.

Levertov publicly opposed the war long before 1968, when her husband, Mitchell Goodman, was indicted with Dr. Benjamin Spock, Michael Ferber, and others, in the first "conspiracy' trial initiated by the U.S. government. The government's various attempts to undermine and to discredit the anti-war movement failed; in addition, activists and writers, in their trials, informed the general public about real, rather than superficial, consequences of that war "reported" in the popular media.

Born October 24, 1923, in Ilford, Essex, England, Denise Levertov moved to the U.S. in 1947 and became a citizen in 1955. Her father was an Anglican clergyman—a convert from Hasidic Judaism, and her mother was a Welsh descendant of the prophet Angel Jones, Levertov published her first collection of poems, *The Double Image*, in 1946, since followed by over forty books of poetry, prose, and translation. Recognized as a major poet of the Post-modernist period, she has taught at colleges and universities throughout the country—eventually retiring from Stanford University—and has received numerous awards and honorary degrees in recognition of her achievement.

After living in New England, Levertov moved to Seattle in the 1980s, while continuing to give frequent public readings, and publishing new collections of poetry and prose. Her longer works include "Mass for the Feast of St. Thomas Didymus" and *El Salvador—Requiem and Invocation*, an oratorio set to music, about the U.S.-financed war against the poor in that Central American country. Until her death in 1997, Denise Levertov maintained an active commitment to justice and peace organizations, supporting them with benefit readings.

A persistent theme in Levertov's prose and poetry is the artist's place in society and the individual's responsibilities for the common good. As with other contemporary artists, Levertov has decried the effect of Cold War rhetoric, its poisoning of the moral atmosphere. Through her poems, a reader senses the grief, fury, and despair that has accompanied this corruption of language. In emphasizing the need for a revitalization of language as a requirement for social change, Levertov agrees with Virginia Woolf's statement, in another context: "My sympathies were all on the side of life." And Levertov's poetry is a powerful source of inspiration and **69** encouragement for "constructing peace" in a violent era.

One of the great achievements of her work is exhibited in her poems on religious themes, "Annunciation," for example, and others on Julian of Norwich and Brother Lawrence. Because of her success in conveying religious insights, without pomposity or rhetoric, Levertov is regarded as one of the great religious poets in English, along with John Donne and George Herbert.

In a large body of work, Levertov's "Life at War" from *The Sorrow Dance* (1967) and "Making Peace" from *Breathing the Water* (1984) are haunted by the effects of war and violence on contemporary culture. Both poems bring together personal and social concerns—private life and public issues-that have haunted writers particularly since 1914.

The initial reference-point in "Life at War" is a statement by Rainer Maria Rilke during the First World War, followed by a lament that "the same war continues." The speaker describes our loss of hope at a time when our memories, even the membranes of our bodies, carry remnants of perpetual war:

> We have breathed the grits of it in, all our lives
> our lungs are pocked with it,
> the mucous membrane of our dreams
> coated with it, the imagination
> filmed over with the gray filth of it.

In direct conflict with this knowledge is the poet's awareness of another humankind, "whose flesh responds to a caress, whose eyes/are flowers that perceive the stars,/whose music excels the music of birds." Which of these definitions of humankind will prevail, the poem asks? Which language will we choose to speak?

Throughout her later years, Levertov struggled to find appropriate responses to these questions. Endeavoring to keep things whole, she has refused to surrender to that dissociation of sensibility that separates the individual person from the common life of all.

"O, language, mother of thought," she asked in "Staying Alive," are you rejecting us as we reject you?" George Orwell posed that question initially, just after the Second World War, as have writers of the Post-modernist period in confronting lies and violence justified by "politics and the English language" over the past fifty years.

Through "a religious devotion to the truth, to the splendor of the authentic," as Levertov once put it, she has named and confronted these injustices, imagined a better future, and occasionally given it exotic form in poetry. A vision of that possible future, arising out of contemplation and action, is evoked in "Making Peace," quoted above, "About Political Action in Which Each Individual Acts from the Heart":

> When solitaries draw close, releasing
> each solitude into its blossoming,
> when we give to each other the roses
> of our communion—
> a culture of gardens, horticulture not agribusiness,
> arbors among the lettuce, small terrains—
> when we taste in small victories sometimes
> the small, ephemeral yet joyful
> harvest of our striving,
> great power flows from us,
> luminous, a promise. Yes! ... Then
> great energy flows from solitude,
> and great power from communion.

By Denise Levertov

Breathing the Water. New York: New Directions, 1988.
Candles in Babylon. New York: New Directions, 1982.
New and Selected Essays. New York: New Directions, 1992.
Selected Poems. New York: New Directions, 2002.

About Denise Levertov

Bly, Robert and David Ray. *A Poetry Reading Against the Vietnam War.* Madison, Minn.: The Sixties Press, 1966.
Breslin, James E.B. *From Modern to Contemporary American Poetry 1945-1965.* Chicago: University of Chicago Press, 1984.

Denise Levertov: Selected Criticism, Vietnam Vortex, Ed. Albert Gelpi. Ann Arbor: University of Michigan Press, 1993.

Mersmann, James F. *Out of the Vietnam Vortex: A Study of Poets and Poetry Against the War*. Lawrence: University Press of Kansas, 1974.

The Letters of Robert Duncan and Denise Levertov, Ed. Robert J. Bertholf and Albert Gelpi. Stanford University Press, 2004.

Daniel Berrigan (1921-)
Philip Berrigan (1923-2002)

In an elegy for his father, written in Danbury Federal Prison during Holy Week, 1972, Daniel Berrigan also sketched his own portrait, an outline of a complex and talented person under the influence of a somewhat distant parent. The poem describes his father's fierce shortcomings, as well as his rich legacy to six sons:

> He exacted performance, promptitude,
> deference to his moods
> the family escutcheon stained with no shit.
> The game was skillful (we never saw it so well played
> elsewhere), he was commonly considered
> the epitome of a just man.
> We sat on our perches blinking like six marmosets. There
> were scenes worthy of Conrad;
> the decks shuddering;
> the world coming to an end. . . .

The expression on the face of the marmoset, a wide-eyed, unblinking creature, astonished by what's coming next, is recognizable as Daniel Berrigan's own. One has seen it in numerous photographs of him: at a demonstration, during a trial, from a pulpit, and at his arrest at Block Island after the months underground in 1970. It is a face that says, "Well, what do you know? Look what I've gotten myself in for this time: The Lord be praised."

An early poem conveys that sense of wonder and the singular manner that characterizes Father Berrigan. "Each day writes/in my heart's core/ineradicably, what it is to be man":

> I tread my earth amazed: what land,
> what skies are these, whose shifting weathers
> now shrink my harvest to a stack of bones;
> now weigh my life with glory?
> Christ. . . your presence give
> light to my eyeless mind, reason to my heart's rhyme.

For all his public activities, as poet, teacher, theologian, war resister, liturgist, Daniel Berrigan is a surprisingly private person. Since his eighteenth year, his vocation as Jesuit and priest has been the center of his life.

Born in 1921, in Minnesota, to Thomas and Frida Bromhart Berrigan, an Irish railroad man with a flair for poetry and drama, and a devout but willful German woman, Daniel Berrigan and his younger brother, Philip, born two years later, attended parochial schools in Syracuse, New York, after their family moved to a farm near there in the 1920s. Daniel's entry into the Society of Jesus (Jesuits) in 1939 preceded the later religious vocations of his older brother Jerome and his younger brother Philip after the Second World War.

The confined, quasi-militarist regime of the Jesuits surprised Daniel, but he did well as a student and began publishing poems in national periodicals while still in college. Soon after his ordination as a priest in 1942, he taught French and English in Jesuit high schools in New Jersey and in Brooklyn, before joining the theology department at Lemoyne College, East Syracuse, in 1957. On a sabbatical leave in 1964, he served as a parish priest in France, where he had studied previously; he admired the worker-priest movement. In further

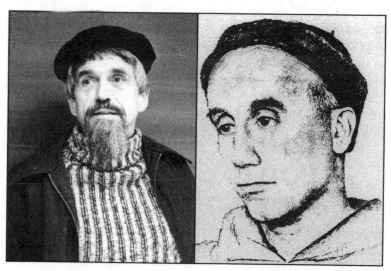

Daniel Berrigan   Thomas Merton

Mulford Sibley   Dorothy Day

travel at this time behind the Iron Curtain, he found the church persecuted, but clear about its religious mission. Back in the United States, where his brother Philip had become involved in the Civil Rights movement, Daniel co-founded several national organizations opposed to the war in Vietnam. Disciplined by the church hierarchy in New York for these activities, he was exiled to South America, which only deepened his resistance to United States policies toward the Third World.

Returning home after six weeks, Daniel became a controversial figure again by his acts of revolutionary nonviolence and through his influence on young people, former students and admirers who eventually followed him into jail for burning draft records. Over the next forty years, Father Berrigan participated in numerous symbolic actions against the state, including the damaging of nuclear weapons systems, the subject of a film, In the *King of Prussia* (1982). He and his brother Philip were an inspiration for activists resisting the deployment of American nuclear missiles in Western Europe.

As a writer, Daniel Berrigan occupies a special place in American letters. In spite of his honors, including the Lamont Poetry Prize in 1957, awarded to an outstanding first book by the Academy of American Poets, as well as the Meltzer, St. Thomas More, and Obie awards, he is seldom treated seriously as an artist by influential critics.. "Writing was as integral to his life in prison as counseling or rapping, or organizing, or listening to the anguish of a prison brother," Philip Berrigan wrote in the introduction to Daniel's *Prison Poems*.

Some readers regard Berrigan's perpetual testing of the boundaries of experience, his effrontery to good behavior, as mere personal orneriness. And, to be sure, there is a bit of the Modernist spirit, the impulse "to shake up the bourgeois," about his style.

Yet it is this quality of expecting the unexpected and his refusal to accept traditional boundaries that accounts in part for Daniel Berrigan's hold on people's attention. Faced, like Herman Melville's Bartleby with the inevitable (in Berrigan's case, obeying the law, paying war taxes, and tolerating

America's policy of Mutually Assured Destruction—MAD), he "prefers not to."

As an artist and activist, Daniel Berrigan promises, in typical American fashion, the unexpected, the impossible. Who else would leave a job at Cornell University (in 1968), fly to Hanoi to rescue three American flyers, return to a small suburb of Baltimore to burn draft records with homemade napalm, go through a long trial, and then, in costume to evade the FBI, slip underground? Narrowly escaping accidental death in prison, he embarked soon afterward on another series of nonviolent actions, smashing missile warheads and risking jail numerous times while out on appeal. This is attended, along the way, by an outpouring of poems, essays, letters to periodicals, an award-winning play, several films, numerous lectures, and religious retreats, a variety of jobs (an orderly in a cancer hospital, and teaching assignments at leading universities) and close associations with a multitude of friends, family, and fellow resisters in this country and Europe.

If, as Wordsworth said, "the child is father of the man," some insight into Daniel Berrigan is provided by the self-portrait mentioned earlier. Equally significant is the famous statement of the Catonsville Nine, in 1968, beginning, "The violence stops here, and death stops here, this war stops here."

> We shall beyond doubt be placed behind bars for some portion of our natural lives in consequence of our inability to live and die content in the plagued city, to say "peace, peace" when there is no peace, to keep the poor poor, the thirsty and hungry thirsty and hungry. Our apologies good friends for the fracture of good order, the burning of paper instead of children, the angering of the orderlies in the front parlor of the charnel house. We could not, so help us God, do otherwise.

The last statement—that he "could not do otherwise"—suggests that, unlike other figures in the history of American radicalism, who chose their fates, Daniel Berrigan regards his as a given. Is this the reason for his rather "Zen" attitude toward it all?

77

For Philip, as well as for Daniel, their father—strong-minded, but alternately romantic and fierce—was a major influence. The poverty and hardship experienced by the family, as well as the strong religious commitment, remained the bedrock of Philip's commitment to social justice and, later, nonviolence.

After completing high school in Syracuse, he had enrolled at St. Michael's College, University of Toronto, before being drafted into the army in 1943 and serving in Europe. "I was Philip the Bold, son of Thomas the Brave, toughest Irish-American kid on the block," he wrote in his autobiography; "more ignorant, I know now, than brave."

Returning home, he entered the College of the Holy Cross, graduating in 1950, and soon after entering the Josephites, a Catholic religious order with a special ministry to African Americans. Teaching at an all-black high school and serving in a parish in Louisiana from 1955 to 1962, he became involved in the civil rights movement. Refused permissions by his religious superiors to participate in Freedom Rides in the early 1960s, he eventually joined his brother, Daniel, in the Selma March of 1965. Disciplined for his outspoken views when he taught at the Josephite seminary in Newburgh, New York, Philip was ordered to pack up and move to St. Peter Claver Church, Baltimore, in the heart of the African American district.

In 1967, when Philip and three others poured blood on draft files and afterward joined his brother Daniel and seven others in burning draft files, the Berrigans helped to move the Catholic population from supporting the war in Vietnam, to active resisting it. For their civil disobedience, they spent two years in federal prisons, including Danbury, Connecticut. During this period, Philip Berrigan and Elizabeth McAlister pledged themselves to one another, announcing their marriage after his release from prison in 1973 and establishing the Jonah House resistance community in Baltimore.

Over the next the three decades, Philip and Elizabeth chronicled the struggles of building and maintaining a resistance community in their writings. They acknowledged that the on-going effort to balance community conscience and individual conscience, while avoiding to "dogmatizing the first and suppressing the second."

Since its founding, Jonah House has harbored a succession of activists who dig graves and smear ashes and blood on the steps of the Pentagon and, since 1980, symbolically disarm weapons of mass destruction on military bases and at arms manufacturers. Just as the draft board raids inspired many young Catholics to similar acts throughout the U.S., a Plowshares action at a General Electric plant in King of Prussia, Pennsylvania, has led to over eighty similar actions in various states and in several foreign countries. In the midst of it all, during extended periods when either Philip and Elizabeth were in prison, they reared three children—Frida, Jerry, and Kate, spoke frequently to varied audiences, conducted retreats, and organized annual protests at the Pentagon on Good Friday and the Feast of the Holy Innocents.

In the history of nonviolence in the United States, Philip Berrigan occupies a special place, with resemblances to and significant differences from abolitionists, labor organizers, and war resisters in American history, largely because of his Catholic heritage. As with earlier figures committed to nonviolent social change, he went through a kind of conversion that redirected his life and priorities as a religious person. Gradually, he turned to activists and writers critical of American foreign and domestic policy, writing in religious periodicals and books about segregation, then the implications of modern warfare and the need to stand against it.

1965, a pivotal year for the Civil Rights movement and American involvement in Vietnam—when Daniel co-founded Clergy and Laity Concerned About Vietnam and was exiled to Latin America—was also a pivotal year for Philip. From then until his death in 2002, he spent eleven years in confinement in numerous courtrooms and jails throughout the United States for civil disobedience.

For a person who confessed his ignorance and docility as a young man, including his ignorance of what Dorothy Day called "the whole rotten system" and the complicity of the institutional Church, Philip Berrigan became a major voice for   79 victims of injustice and an instrument of reform, indeed of nonviolent revolution. In his mature years, as an irritant to the war-making State and its apologists, this truly great man lived a demanding religious vocation, often joining his brother, Daniel, in projecting images of hope in a dark time.

By Daniel Berrigan

And the Risen Bread: Selected Poems, Ed. John Dear. Fordham University Press, 1998.

Daniel Berrigan: Poetry, Drama, Prose, Ed. Michael True. Maryknoll, NY: Orbis Books, 1988.

Lights on in the House of the Dead: A Prison Diary. New York: Doubleday and Co., 1974.

Prison Poems. Greensboro, N.C.: Unicorn Press, 1973.

To Dwell in Peace: An Autobiography. New York: Harper and Row, 1985.

By Philip Berrigan

A Punishment for Peace. New York: Macmillan, 1969.

Fighting the Lamb's War: Skirmishes With the American Empire: The Autobiography of Philip Berrigan, with Fred Wilcox. Monroe, ME: Common Courage Press, 1996.

Prison Journals of A Priest Revolutionary. New York: Holt, Rinehart, and Winston, 1970.

The Time's Discipline: The Beatitudes and Nuclear Resistance. with Elizabeth McAlister. Baltimore, MD: Fortkamp Publishers, 1989.

About the Berrigans

Polner, Murray, and Jim Grady. *Disarmed and Dangerous: The Radical Life and Times of Daniel and Philip Berrigan.* New York: Basic Books, 1997.

Wilcox, Fred. *Uncommon Martyrs: The Plowshares Movement and the Catholic Left.* Reading, MA: Addison-Wesley Publishing Co., 1991.

Howard Zinn (1922-)

In Howard Zinn, democracy has its American historian, a writer and teacher attuned to the forces that just might create a world with respect for equality and human rights. Unlike many historians, he fixes attention not on wars and government, but on the ideas, imagination, and courage of ordinary people. And in a host of articles, essays, and books published since 1959, he focuses on acts of disobedience and solidarity of the past two centuries that initiated mass movements for liberation. Confronted with such large popular movements against injustice, the established order—and sometimes even the state—has given way to reason and reform.

In charting this history, Howard Zinn commits something more than his voice and tenure as an academic, beginning with his active involvement in the civil rights movement and in resistance to the draft, the nuclear arms race, and the war on Iraq. With a handful of talented and committed academics and artists, including Noam Chomsky, Grace Paley, Denise Levertov, George Wald, and Richard Falk, Zinn makes the link between scholarship and humane values, between the academy and the public order. He is, in fact, almost a National Endowment for the Humanities himself.

Born in New York City on August 24, 1922, Zinn has lived in the Boston area, with his wife and family, since 1964. He, like many men of his generation, "grew up" in the armed services, and was decorated as an air force bombardier in Europe during the Second World War. Afterward, he completed his formal education at New York University and Columbia University under the G.I. bill, receiving a Ph.D. in history in 1958. Before moving to Boston University, he chaired the history and social science department at Spellman College, in Atlanta; during those years, he was also deeply involved in the civil rights movement and wrote an important study of the Student Nonviolent Coordinating Committee, SNCC: The New Abolitionists (1964).

Prior to the publication of his major work, *A People's History of the United States* (1980), Zinn wrote frequently on politics and the social thought of the Great Depression and on the tradition of civil disobedience in American history. In February 1968, he, with Father Daniel Berrigan, arranged the release of three American prisoners of war in North Vietnam, during a special visit to that country. Since that time, Zinn has testified on behalf of people on trial for resisting the draft or for damaging nuclear weapons equipment; he has appeared in numerous films, such as *Holy Outlaw* (1970) and *Lovejoy's Nuclear War* (1976), that dramatize those issues. He is the author, as well, of a successful biographical drama about Karl Marx (*Marx in Soho*) and Emma Goldman (*Emma*), anarchist and feminist.

In writing history, Zinn has taken his lead not from the announced purposes of governments, but from their actions, their deeds. He has been careful, for example, to note "the warring elements" of the American creed. By this he means a conflict between the rhetorical creed, represented by the Declaration of Independence ("all Men are created equal," the right to revolution, and so on) and the working creed. The hard evidence is

that all men are created equal, except foreigners with whom we are at war, blacks who have not been signaled out for special attention, Indians who will not submit, inmates of prisons, members of the armed forces, and anyone without money.

In his writings, as well as in his undergraduate classes and public lectures, Zinn spells out the consequences of this dichotomy, especially America's failure to alter its allocation of power and wealth. He occasionally admits that changes take place within the narrow boundaries of profit-motivated capitalism, a paternalistic political system, an aggressive foreign policy, and "a social system based on a culture of prejudices concerning race, national origin, sex, age, and wealth."

Zinn's truths are obvious to many observers outside the United States, but few people profess them "inside the whale," and even fewer from the hallowed groves of academe. Although his view of history is sometimes regarded as unorthodox, his authority as a teacher and written has won him a wide audience among students and scholars, as well as a significant, permanent place among modern historians. With E.P. Thompson, in England, Zinn has made the history of the working class visible in a way that it has seldom been since the 1930s, at least.

> First, why did the United States, exactly as it became the most heavily armed and wealthiest society in the world, run into so much trouble with its own people? From the late fifties to the early seventies, the nation experienced unprecedented black rebellion, student demonstrations, anti-war agitation, civil disobedience, prison uprising, and a widespread feeling that American civilization was faltering, or even in decay. And second, what are the possibilities, the visions, the beginnings of fresh directions for this country?

Decades later, Zinn continues to explore the implications of these radical questions. In the same quiet, measured voice, with an understated, even wry humor, he lectures to large audiences, speaks at a rallies against war, on the Boston Common, and addresses meetings of professional historians and political scientists. Patient and persistent, he appears **83** confident that his message will get through, amid the conventional noise and chatter. In the long effort to get the facts straight and to keep alive the history of ordinary people, he behaves as if time were on his side, "as long," he might add, "as the bomb doesn't fall."

By Howard Zinn

A People's History of the United States: 1492-Present. New York: Harper and Row, 1980.

The Politics of History. Boston: The Beacon Press, 1970.

Disobedience and Democracy. New York: Random House, 1968.

SNCC: The New Abolitionists. Boston: The Beacon Press, 1964.

You Can't Be Neutral on a Moving Train: A Personal History of Our Times. Boston: Beacon Press, 1994.

The Zinn Reader: Writings on Disobedience and Democracy. New York: Seven Stories Press, 1997.

Voices of the People's History of the United States, with Anthony Arnove. New York: Seven Stories Press, 2004.

Kenneth Boulding (1910-93)
Elise Boulding (1920-)

Elise Boulding has described the modest beginnings of the International Peace Research Association (IPRA) in as "a small group of participants from different continents talking about how they could support one another in turning heir scientific knowledge to the elimination of war." With her husband, Kenneth Boulding, and others providing a theoretical base, scholars from Europe, Asia, Africa, and the Americas gradually aligned their efforts for "positive peace" with their vocations as teachers and researchers.

Kenneth and Elise Boulding met in the spring of 1941 at a gathering where she was "taken into membership by the Society of Friends (Quakers)," she wrote forty-eight years later. In the meantime, their achievement in writing, teaching, and organizing has led to Nobel prize nominations, he in economics and she for peace. By their activism and their scholarship, as co-founders of IPRA, which she has served as executive secretary, and its North American affiliate, the Consortium on Peace Research, Education and Development (COPRED), now known as Peace and Justice Studies Association, the couple has influenced the lives of many people, especially teachers and researchers in peace and world security studies.

Born in Oslo, July 6, 1920, Elise Bjorn-Hansen moved to the United States as a young woman, graduated from Douglass College, and in 1941 married Kenneth Boulding. Though a committed pacifist, she looked to Kenneth, ten years older, "as teacher/companion/guide" in peacemaking. While rearing five children and becoming involved in movements for social change ("I began working for peace there, in the context of family and community."), she completed graduate study at Iowa State University and the University of Michigan, wrote for professional journals, and eventually served as Secretary General of the Women's International League for Peace and Freedom and the International Peace Research Association. As a sociologist, she taught at the University of Colorado, Boulder, then later at Dartmouth College. "The scholar-activist dichotomy has never been an issue for me," she has said. "There is nothing without practice, and data is useless without experientially grounded models that can show how facts inter-relate."

Integrating means and ends, in working for peace, has been a preoccupation of Elise Boulding since the beginning. "The way we work is as important as the issues on which we work," she told the vice president of Pax Christi International. "Each of us must choose a focus, but unless we keep in mind the connections, our work loses its relevance." Influenced by Fred Polac, a Dutch author whose book she translated, she agrees with him that society moves toward "the future it envisions." Elise Boulding's major books are replete with essential insights related to the "new" inter-discipline and provided language and concepts that are central to the United Nations Decade for the Culture of Peace and Nonviolence for the Children of the World, passed by 169 nations of the General Assembly in 1999.

Kenneth Boulding's major contribution to peace research is at once subtle and deep, reflecting the wide intellectual interests and competencies of the man. Uncompromising in his commitment to peace, he recognized, nonetheless, the deficiency in its social theory, which led to "frequent break-downs" interrupting the progress of the movement. Much of his scholarly writing arose from a conviction "that the intellectual chassis of the broad movement for the abolition of war has not been adequate to support the powerful moral engine which drives it." For that reason particularly, he has worked to improve the theoretical and intellectual underpinnings of structures for peace. His *Stable Peace* (1978), based upon lectures at the University of Texas, is perhaps his most skillful, readable reflection on the nature of such structures.

Economist, teacher, author, and pacifist, Kenneth Ewart Boulding is a native of Liverpool, England, where he was born January 18, 1910. Reared a Methodist, he found in the Quaker meeting in Liverpool, and later at Oxford, a place where religious experience complemented "his deepening intellectual grasp of the world." Planning to study chemistry, he eventually settled on economics, and after completing undergraduate and graduate degrees at Oxford University, received a faculty appointment at the University of Edinburgh, Scotland. Invited to teach at Colgate University during a visit to the United States in 1937, then taught at many universities in this country and abroad, for a number of years at the University of Michigan and from 1980, until his death in 1993, at the University of Colorado, Boulder.

Early on, living his pacifist principles got Boulding into trouble. In 1942, for example, he lost a job as a staff member with the League of Nations Economic and Financial Section, in New Jersey, for circulating a statement asking people to give up their national allegiances and to cast away their weapons. In 1948, he waged a legal battle to become a naturalized U.S. citizen without taking the oath to bear arms. An activist/academic, he initiated campaigns against nuclear testing and the draft, refused to sign stringent loyalty oaths during the McCarthy era, and supported movements for social change in body as well as in principle. All of these tasks were accomplished, his associates say, with good humor and with time for **87** writing sonnets that mark the principal occasions of his life.

The inspiration for and the origins of Elise and Kenneth Boulding's combined effort for peace were his passionate conviction as a youth "that war was the major moral and intellectual problem of our age"; and her realization in 1940, when Hitler invaded Norway, her native country, "that the only way to have security is to have it for everyone." An early cooperative venture was the Center for Conflict Resolution at the University of Michigan, which Kenneth helped to initiate and Elise served as volunteer secretary/editor/networker in the late 1950s and early 1960s. About the same time, Students for a Democratic Society, involving some of their Michigan students, issued the Port Huron Statement, followed soon afterward by the first teach-ins against the Vietnam war.

In post-World War Two America, when universities were often co-opted by the war-making state in the service of the C.I.A. or the Pentagon, Kenneth Boulding's priorities were ignored by most academics. Cold War rhetoric, in its attempts "to make lies sound truthful and murder respectable and to give the appearance of solidity to pure wind," as Orwell said in 1947, left little room for talk of peace research, as many scholars enlisted in—or tolerated the inanities of—the military-industrial- university complex.

In his manner of conducting himself, as citizen and scholar, Boulding offered an alternative to academic Cold Warriors embracing the politics of the moment. Long before university presidents from around the world spoke, in their 1989 Talloires Declaration, of the need for "language, history, culture, and methods to create peace," and before the American bishops, in their 1983 pastoral letter, urged Catholic universities "to develop programs for rigorous, interdisciplinary research, education and training directed toward peacemaking expertise," Boulding had begun that painstaking, moral, and intellectual effort.

The Bouldings' active involvement in the issues of their time helped to keep the new discipline of peace studies from becoming just another trendy discipline, "merely academic." "Despairing of protest, others have turned toward violence, but he has turned toward knowledge," Cynthia Kerman, Kenneth's

biographer, says. And the Bouldings' projects and publications—poetry, religious reflections, economic and sociological
treatises—have earned them public recognition, including
many honorary degrees and reputations as two of the essential
social scientists of our time.

By the early 1970s, the Bouldings were cooperating with
other scholars committed to "education for an interdependent
world": Herbert Kelman, who co-edited the *Journal of Conflict
Resolution*, founded in 1957, and later directed the Harvard
Program on Negotiation; Chadwick Alger, Ohio State
University; Bernice Carroll, Purdue University; Betty Reardon,
Teacher's College, Columbia University, for example, and
Anatol Rapoport, Canada; Johan Galtung, Norway; and
Yoshikazu Sakamoto, Japan. As peace researchers, they recognized the various instabilities "resulting from the Cold War era
and the failure of Western-based development strategies," as
Elise Boulding told the twenty-fifth annual IPRA conference in
Groningen, the Netherlands, in 1990. Since 1965, participation
at such meetings, on weapons technology, human rights,
nonviolence, and ecology, had increased from 71 people from
22 countries, to 341 people from 57 countries, in an organization
numbering 1000 members. By 2000, over three hundred
colleges and universities in the U.S. offered courses and
programs in peace studies, including graduate programs at the
Syracuse, George Mason, and Eastern Mennonite, and Notre
Dame universities. Other major programs are offered at
Bradford University, England, and University of Queensland,
Australia, as well as peace research centers in Germany.
Norway, Denmark, and Sweden.

In a verse-prophecy—one of many good-natured poetic
responses to changing times, Kenneth Boulding once described
IPRA and COPRED as attempts to integrate

> Research and Training, in one wise
> And fruitful kind of enterprise.

By 1990, these goals informed a number of graduate and
undergraduate programs in peace studies and conflict   **89**
resolution, as well as publicly funded in public programs in

Ohio, Kentucky and New York. "COPRED cannot claim all the credit,/But still it made more plus than debit," Boulding rightly observed, emphasizing the hard "peacework" yet to be done:

And if we don't get up and do it,
Somebody's surely going to rue it.
And things may go from bad to worse,
Like this incessant doggerel verse.

By Kenneth and Elise Boulding

Boulding, Elise, *Building a Global Civil Culture: Education for an Interdependent World*. Syracuse: Syracuse University Press, 1990.

—. *Cultures of Peace: The Hidden Side of History*. Syracuse University Press, 2000.

Boulding, Kenneth. *Sonnets from the Interior Life and Other Biographical Verse*. Boulder, Col.: Colorado Associated University Press, 1975.

—. *Stable Peace*. Austin: University of Texas Press, 1976.

About Kenneth and Elise Boulding

Frontiers in Social Thought: Essays in Honor of Kenneth E. Boulding. Ed. Martin Pfaff, North-Holland, 1976.

Kerman, Cynthia. *Creative Tension: The Life and Thought of Kenneth Boulding*. Ann Arbor: University of Michigan Press, 1974.

Morrison, Mary Lee. *Elise Boulding: A Life in the Cause of Peace*. Jefferson, NC: McFarland and Co., 2005.

Oscar Romero (1917-80)

Romero, perhaps the most powerful religious film I have ever seen, introduced many people in the United States to the life of Oscar Romero, and suggested why his example informs the hearts and minds of millions, particularly in Latin America and the Third World. In less than a decade, he has joined the company of Gandhi and Martin Luther King as an inspiration and guide in the struggle for human rights and nonviolent social change. In time, he may be canonized.

When he was consecrated archbishop of San Salvador in 1977, Oscar Romero appeared a safe choice—timid, scholarly, "spiritual." Moderate in his opinions and critical of liberation theologians, Romero was regarded as "a compromise candidate" among the native clergy, someone who would neither challenge nor upset the ruling oligarchy of El Salvador. In this smallest, most densely populated country of Central America—on the Pacific Ocean, between Guatemala and Honduras—the rich owned 80 percent of the land, and the army, with U.S. military equipment and training, enforced the status quo by terrorizing workers and landless peasants.

In his first letter to fellow clergy, shortly after festivities marking his consecration, Romero spoke in traditional—

abstract, though hardly platitudinous—language about a religious faith "that identifies us with the one priesthood of Christ ... and all the human virtues that nourish our supernatural communion on the natural and psychological levels."

Three years later, when he lay dead in a convent chapel, after being shot while saying Mass, people looked back at that earlier letter. Jon Sobrino, a Jesuit theologian in Romero's diocese who had had reservations about his appointment as archbishop, reflected on the younger Romero: "His theology was questionable. Beyond question, however, was his profound faith in God, and his surpassing concern for the glory of God in this world." In the intervening years, Oscar Romero's perspective on what constituted "the glory of God in this world" had changed. Some called that change "a conversion"; others regarded it as a natural consequence of his concern for and dedication to his people in a dangerous time.

Whatever the reasons for it, his altered perspective had profound implications for the church in El Salvador and the response of the ruling oligarchy toward that institution. In a speech that Romero gave one month before he was murdered, he described the profound implications of his change for the poor, for theology, for the church (the translation is Philip Berryman's):

> We believe in Jesus
> who came to give life in abundance
> and we believe in a living God
> who gives life to human beings
> and wants them to truly live.
> These radical truths of faith
> become real truths...
> when the church involves itself
> in the life and death of its people.
> So the church,
> like every person,
> is faced with the most basic option for its faith,
> being for life or death....
> on this point there is no possible neutrality.
> We either serve the life of Salvadorans

or we are accomplices in their death....
We either believe in a God of life
or we serve the idols of death.

Re-reading Romero's words during this tense period and knowing the price he paid for uttering them make one wonder at the courage that sustained him.

Born August 15, 1917, in eastern El Salvador, near the Honduran border, Oscar Amulfo Romero was the second child of Santos Romero and Guadalupe de Jesus Galdamez. Leaving home at thirteen, where he worked as a carpenter's apprentice, he made a seven-hour trip by horseback in order to enter the minor seminary at San Miguel. At twenty, he transferred to the national seminary in San Salvador before being sent to Rome, where he was ordained a priest in 1942.

Returning to his own diocese in El Salvador for the next twenty-five years, Romero gained a reputation as a kind but demanding priest. In 1967, he was transferred to the capital city of San Salvador, and later, as auxiliary bishop, was assigned to secondary tasks. Generally sympathetic, like many Latin American bishops, to the historic realignment of the Catholic church toward the poor after the Second Vatican Council, Romero was nonetheless close to priests associated with Opus Dei and critical of liberation theology.

As bishop of his old diocese in the early 1970s, according to one of his priests, Romero quoted documents of the Second Vatican Council; but he never referred to those of Medellin, by Latin American bishops. In 1977, although many clergy probably preferred his contemporary Arturo Rivera Damas, Romero was named successor to Archbishop Luis Chavez y Gonzalez, who had sided with working people in their efforts for better wages and working conditions.

Speaking always for peaceful reform, Romero soon had to face the fact, as a national leader, that the government made no distinction between people working for nonviolent social change and those advocating violent revolution. In the eyes of state officials, everyone for reform was "a doctrinaire Marxist," including nuns and priests teaching in Catholic schools; and uniformed soldiers or secret death squads killed increasing

93

numbers of human-rights activists, students, and technicians, as well as urban guerillas armed against the oligarchy.

Only weeks after his consecration as archbishop, Romero had to officiate at the funeral of Father Rutilio Grande, a personal friend and master of ceremonies at Romero's episcopal ordination. A popular priest, whose sermons denounced the exploitation of the many by the few, Grande, along with a young boy and an old man, was murdered as he drove a jeep across the flat sugarcane fields, one of the few places landless campesinos could find work in his region.

Not long afterward, Romero began to speak more directly about the suffering of his people and the proper response of Christians to that condition. "A church that does not unite itself to the poor in order to denounce from the place of the poor the injustice committed against them is not truly the Church of Jesus Christ," he said. For Romero, the place of the poor in El Salvador became indistinguishable from "the place of the skull," where Christ died, and he increasingly identified their suffering with the suffering of Jesus. In Sunday sermons from the Cathedral in El Salvador, he demanded an accounting of the abuses by the police and an end to the war between the national army and guerillas. And when El Salvador's president offered him protection, Romero, though fearing his own death, answered that rather than his own security, what he wanted was "security and tranquility for 108 families and their 'disappeared,' " adding that a "shepherd seeks no security as long as the flock is threatened."

In a letter to President Jimmy Carter, six weeks before Romero's death, he expressed hope that the president's religious sentiments and sensitivity to human rights would move him to halt U.S. economic and military assistance to the military junta, "thus avoiding greater bloodshed in this suffering country." And on March 23, 1980, the day before Romero was murdered, he spoke directly to those primarily responsible for the violence, those under government orders:

94

We are your people. The peasants you kill are your own brothers and sisters. When you hear the voice of the man commanding you to kill, remember instead the voice of

God. Thou Shalt Not Kill.... No soldier is obliged to obey an order contrary to the law of God. There is still time for you to obey your conscience, even in the face of a sinful command to kill.

The church, defender of the rights of God, of the law of God, and the dignity of each human being, cannot remain silent in the presence of such abominations. In the name of God, in the name of our tormented people whose cries rise up to Heaven, I beseech you, I beg you, I command you, stop the repression.

Decades after his death, Romero's spirit is more alive than ever among those working at home and abroad to alleviate the violence, including ending U.S. military intervention in Central America. Ignoring Romero, the Carter administration—but more cynically, the Reagan and Bush administrations—made every citizen of the U.S. complicit in the deaths of seventy thousand people in El Salvador. Those murdered included citizens of the U.S., such as Sisters Maura Clarke, M.M., Ita Ford, M.M., Dorothy Kazel, O.S.U., and Jean Donovan, who were killed eight months after Romero. Not until six Jesuit priests and two women were murdered, similarly, in 1989 did the U.S. government seriously reconsider its massive aid to the Salvadoran military, then second only to U.S. aid to Israel.

"The word remains. This is the great comfort of one who preaches," Romero said in a 1978 homily. "My voice will disappear, but my word, which is Christ, will remain." Whatever peace comes to El Salvador and whatever hope landless, impoverished peasants enjoy owes a debt to the theology of Oscar Romero and to the ultimate sacrifice that it required of him.

By Oscar Romero

Voice of the Voiceless: The Four Pastoral Letters and Other Statements. Maryknoll, N.Y.: Orbis Books, 1985.

About Oscar Romero

Berryman, Phillip. *The Religious Roots of Rebellion: Christians in Central American Revolutions*. Maryknoll, N.Y.: Orbis Books, 1984.

Brockman, James R., S.J. *The Word Remains: A Life of Oscar Romero*. Maryknoll, N.Y.: Orbis Books, 1982.

Sobrino, Jon. *Archbishop Romero: Memories and Reflections*. Tr. Robert R. Barr, Maryknoll, N.Y.: Orbis Books, 1990.

Thomas Merton (1915-68)

Although he lived much of his adult life cloistered as a Trappist monk, Thomas Merton was partly responsible for the emergence of an active community for nonviolent social change among American Catholics; he prodded, even provoked them out of a kind of social torpor. Before the mid-sixties, few American Catholics were visible in movements initiated and sustained by civil rights and pacifist groups—the National Association for the Advancement of Colored People (NAACP), for example, or historic peace churches or organizations.

Through the influence of Dorothy Day and the Catholic Worker movement and the writings of Merton and Gordon Zahn, American Catholics began to join and eventually to initiate activist groups addressing a range of issues related to civil rights and nuclear disarmament. By 1970, they were visible as "the Catholic conspiracy against the war," as Zahn called it, and formidable enough to provoke the ire of fellow communicant J. Edgar Hoover, the politically powerful head of the Federal Bureau of Investigation. Other important contributors to a change in attitude among American Catholics were the Second Vatican Council (1962-65); John XXIII, its initiator; and his encyclicals *Mater et Magistra* and *Pacem in Terris*.

Traditionally working class—as well as liberal and Democratic in their voting record since 1928—Catholics had seldom been central to movements for fundamental social change and never at the center of a peace movement. After 1964, in part because of Thomas Merton, first individual members, then the institutional church, began to change.

The year 1964 is a key time for new currents in Catholic social thought because of several events, including the publication of Gordon Zahn's *In Solitary Witness: The Life and Death of Franz Jagerstatter*, following his important book *German Catholics and Hitler's Wars* two years earlier; the founding of the Catholic Peace Fellowship, by Tom Cornell, James Forest, former editors of the *Catholic Worker*, and Philip Berrigan, a Josephite priest at that time; and a retreat on the "Spiritual Roots of Protest" at the Cistercian (Trappist) Abbey of Our Lady of Gethsemani, Kentucky.

John XXIII's encyclical evoked support for a peace movement, beginning with a major U.N. related conference sponsored by the Center for the Study of Democratic Institutions and involving Robert Hutchins, John Cogley, and a host of internationally known scholars, editors, and political leaders. Similarly, Zahn's biography of Jagerstatter provided a powerful example of a devout Austrian peasant who, like many young Catholic conscientious objectors later on, simply said "No!" to killing—in his case, as a potential member of Hitler's army.

The Trappist retreat, involving Cornell, Forest, Berrigan, and others, included presentations by A.J. Muste, John Howard Yoder, Daniel Berrigan, S.J., and most significantly, Thomas Merton, on "The Monastic Protest: The Voice in the Wilderness." Four years later, several participants were in prison for burning draft files at selective service offices throughout the U.S.

In published notes for "Spiritual Roots of Protest," Merton expressed hope of finding "common grounds for *religious dissent and commitment* in the face of the injustice and disorder of a world in which total war seems at times inevitable...." He sought "not the formulation of a program, but a deepening of

98

roots," when others appeared to be offering only "violent solutions to economic and social problems more critical and more vast than man has ever known before." From his notes, it is clear that Merton had been thinking about, had even been haunted by, these concerns for some time. As recently as 1962, he had joined PAX, a U.S. branch of a British peace organization, had written for and corresponded frequently with editors of the Catholic Worker, and had edited an important anthology, *Breakthrough to Peace*; it included essays by others concerned about the nuclear arms race: Erich Fromm, Lewis Mumford, Norman Cousins, and Gordon Zahn.

Merton's introduction to *Breakthrough to Peace* surveys in a prophetic way the complex moral and spiritual questions that have occupied scientists, ethicists, artists, and theologians ever since. It addresses directly, for example, what Robert Jay Lifton later called "psychic numbing" and what Merton regarded as "secret forces that rise up within us and dictate fatal decisions." Such behavior can only be countered by a morality, a wisdom that permeates "every judgment, every choice, every political act that deserves to be called civilized." To act in that way, Merton added, we must

> shake off our passive irresponsibility, renounce our fatal-
> istic submission to economic and social forces, and give
> up the unquestioning belief in machines and processes
> which characterizes the mass mind.

Four years later, in 1968, the year that Merton died in Bangkok, he wrote another essay that develops a similar theme, with particular reference to the Cold War's corruption of language. As a writer, Merton was angry, as Orwell had been in "Politics and the English Language" (1946), about those who. Orwell said, try "to make lies sound truthful and murder respectable, and to give the appearance of solidity to pure wind." Merton focused on a warrior "language" used to accomplish similar goals: "the pompous and sinister jargon of the war mandarins in government offices and military think-tanks." Generally, Merton's "War and the Crisis of Language" brings together themes informing his other perceptive writings on peace; it also fleshes out his discussion of approaches to social change in an earlier pamphlet, *Blessed Are the Meek: The Christian Roots of Nonviolence*. A lifetime of experience, writing, and reflection had brought him to this point. For that reason, among others, the posthumously published volume *Thomas Merton on Peace* (or *The Nonviolent Alternative*), with Gordon Zahn's introduction, occupies a special place among classic statements on nonviolence.

Born January 31, 1915, in Prades, France, in the Eastern Pyrenees, Merton was the older son of Owen and Ruth Jenkins Merton, a New Zealand painter and an American dancer. His parents had met in Paris four years before "Tom" was born. After his mother died, when he was six years old, he was reared in England, France, and on Long Island. The death of his father during his teenage years—and of his brother in the Second World War—undoubtedly influenced his eventual choice of a vocation, at least up through his early manhood. After entering Clare College, Cambridge University, in 1933, he moved to the U.S., and at Columbia University made a number of close literary friendships—including Robert Giroux and James Laughlin—that remained important the rest of his life. By 1940, he had already published reviews in the New York *Times* and poems in several periodicals.

In 1941, following a conversion to Roman Catholicism at Columbia, Merton left New York for the Trappist monastery in Kentucky, where he was ordained in 1949 as Father M. Louis. His *The Seven Storey Mountain* (1948), a selective autobiography that focused on his conversion, sold 600,000 copies in the original hardcover; admired by Evelyn Waugh and Graham Green, it made Merton internationally famous. After that, he published numerous books of spiritual writings, meditations, poetry, and, in the 1960s, essays on peace and social justice, all of which remain widely read. Over the years, he served as novice master at the monastery and later lived as a hermit. **100** Although he maintained a prodigious correspondence and occasionally visited friends in New York, he spent his remaining years at Gethsemani. In 1968, at 54, he made a fateful trip to Southeast Asia to meet with Buddhist monks and the Dalai Lama, and died as the result of an accident in Thailand. Merton's influence has been acknowledged by a number of the principal figures in Catholic social teaching and action, including Daniel Berrigan, Jim Forest, Ernesto Cardenal—who cite his letters to them as especially important.

Although less significant as works of art, Merton's poems are interesting in foreshadowing ideas and concerns that inform his later essays. "Original Child Bomb" (1961), with its forty-one verses "for meditation to be scratched on the walls of a cave," is one example. A brief history of events leading to Hiroshima, it describes the fascination, even exhilaration with which people involved in making and deploying the bomb responded to it. "What poor, dumb things we are to cooperate so enthusiastically in our own undoing," Merton seems to say.

In meditation 32, he focuses on the explosion itself:

> The fireball was 180,000 feet across. The temperature at the center of the fireball was 100,000,000 degrees. The people who were near the center became nothing. The whole city was blown to bits and the ruins all caught fire instantly everywhere, burning briskly. 70,000 people were killed right away or died within a few hours. Those who did not die at once suffered great pain. Few of them were soldiers.

American airmen, reacting to the event (in meditation 33) "thought of/the people in the city and they were not/perfectly happy. Some felt they had done wrong. But in any case they had obeyed orders. It was war.'" For Merton, more startling than the war mentality that produced the bomb was the religious language used by the Japanese, unknowingly, in naming it ("Original Child" bomb) and by others, knowingly, in reporting its effects (meditation 34):

> Over the radio went the code message that the bomb had been successful: "Visible effects greater than Trinity... Proceeding to Papacy." Papacy was the code name for Tinian.

101

Here and elsewhere, the satiric tone of the verse reflects the irony, sadness, and anger that characterize Merton's later reflections on peace and war.

Much as he loved the church and his religious community—or perhaps because he loved them—he ridicules the pretension and scandal associated with its "just war" theories, its blessing of the cannons. An admired and devoted communicant, he wrote at a time when his interpretation of the implications of Catholic social teachings and obligations were not widely held—indeed, when such views "were highly suspect and, to some of our fellow Catholics, probably on the fringes of heresy," as Gordon Zahn wrote.

Rereading Merton's later writings, particularly, one is struck by their power and simplicity, their honesty and subtlety—achieved, his biographers suggest, at considerable cost to himself. Decades after his death, they remain among our most important writings on nonviolence.

By Thomas Merton

Gandhi on Nonviolence. Ed. Thomas Merton, New York: New Directions, 1965.

The Nonviolent Alternative. Ed. Gordon Zahn. New York: Farrar, Straus, and Giroux, 1971, 1980.

Zen and the Birds of Appetite. New York: New Directions, 1968.

About Thomas Merton

Furlong, Monica. *Merton: A Biography.* San Francisco: Harper & Row, 1980.

Mott, Michael. *The Seven Mountains of Thomas Merton.* Boston: Houghton Mifflin, 1984.

War or Peace? The Search for New Answers. Ed. Thomas Shannon, Maryknoll, N.Y.: Orbis Books, 1980.

David Dellinger (1915-2004)

For a man born into a Republican family who claimed that all he knew about as a young man was "sports and girls," David Dellinger was remarkably unpredictable, even revolutionary. Although his refusal to register for the draft in 1940 is usually cited as the beginning of his activist life as pacifist and socialist, he was already committed, at 25, to justice issues, including efforts to gain political asylum for Jews and antifascists escaping from Hitler's Germany. He had been anti-Nazi in "a naive and inexperienced way," he wrote later, after realizing that the U.S. under Franklin Roosevelt "imposed an arms embargo on democratic Spain," but failed to stop American corporations "shipping oil, scrap iron, and munitions all over the world, including fascist Japan."

The irony of our government's attacking policies of dictatorial governments while supporting them with money and munitions was not lost on the young ministerial student. It's a contradiction that influenced his vocation as one of the most faithful apostles of nonviolence in U.S. history.

Born in Wakefield, Massachusetts, on August 22, 1915, to an educated, conservative New England family, David Dellinger, like his father—a Boston lawyer—graduated from

Yale University. After spending a year at New College, Oxford, he returned to Yale Divinity School. In 1939, he moved to New Jersey as an associate minister and began studies at Union Theological Seminary in nearby New York City.

Already a pacifist, Dellinger was imprisoned in 1940 for a year and a day at Danbury (Conn.) Federal Prison for refusing to register for the newly initiated draft—although he would have qualified for a ministerial deferment at the time. Later he served two years at Lewisburg (PA) Penitentiary, when he would not report for induction into the armed forces or for an assignment at a Civilian Public Service Camp. At Lewisburg, his commitment to social justice led to his initiating a 65-day hunger strike protesting racial segregation. Ending up in "the hole" (solitary confinement), he learned "that there are no comforts, no luxury, no honors, nothing that can compare with having a sense of one's own integrity—one's knowledge that in his own life, in his own commitment, he is living up to the best that he knows."

While his contemporaries were fighting a war with the Japanese or the Germans, Dellinger was engaged in a demanding struggle at home. In many ways, his physical and moral condition resembled that of Karl Shapiro's conscientious objector, in a poem of that title written during Shapiro's years as a soldier in the South Pacific:

> The gates clanged and they walked you into jail
> More tense than felons but relieved to find
> The hostile world shut out...
> A sense of quiet, of pulling down the blind
> Possessed you. Punishment you felt was clean.

Acknowledging the contribution of that "mutinous crew... The opposite of all armies," to which Dellinger belonged, Shapiro concludes the poem with a tribute to war resisters: "Your conscience is/What we come back to in the armistice."

Working briefly as a farm hand and in a factory after his release from prison in 1945, Dellinger spent most of the next two decades "living and working communally" in Newark and in Glen Gardner, New Jersey. In addition to his wife, Elizabeth Peterson, and their five children, his close associates during this period included a "who's who" of advocates for nonviolent social change in the U.S.: A.J. Muste, Bayard Rustin, Paul Goodman, Staughton Lynd, Barbara Deming, Sidney Lens, Marj Swann, Rita and Marty Corbin. Several of them contributed to the periodicals that Dellinger edited and sometimes set in type: *Direct Action, Alternative,* and *Liberation.*

The latter magazine "signaled a new moment in American radical culture and politics, by giving radical pacifism a revolutionary wing," according to Charles DeBenedetti, a leading historian of peace reform movements. In an effort to address "the decline of independent radicalism and the gradual fading into silence of prophetic and rebellious voices" during the Cold War years, Dellinger published important political commentators and artists including Dorothy Day, Michael Harrington, Lewis Mumford, Kenneth Rexroth, and called attention early on to Martin Luther King's leadership in the Civil Rights movement. While editing *Liberation,* Dellinger also worked closely with the War Resisters League and Committee for Nonviolent Action, organizing activities related to disarmament and civil rights.

In the late 1950s, Dellinger joined Ammon Hennacy and others protesting Civil Defense drills in New York City, who argued that the only real defense against nuclear weapons was to stop making them. As a visible and persistent opponent of war, Dellinger served as co-chair of the New Mobilization Committee to End the War in Vietnam and in numerous other key positions in a long, demanding, and ultimately successful campaign. He also traveled to Southeast Asia three times (and again in 1985) and to Paris twice during the war, in important meetings with North Vietnamese officials, including arrangements for the release of American pilots.

The attitude of those responsible for our Vietnam policy toward Dellinger is suggested by Congressman (later President) Gerald Ford's contention that demonstrations against the Vietnam war were "planned and organized in

Hanoi." In one of many efforts to crush the anti-war movement, the U.S. government indicted Dellinger as a member of the Chicago 8 (with Abbie Hoffman, Bobby Seale, Tom Hayden, and others) for conspiring to disrupt the Democratic National Convention in Chicago in 1968. The long and confusing trial was generally characterized by improprieties on the judge's part that led to most of the charges being dismissed; its consequences included the growth of the anti-war movement and considerable public acclaim for the defendants.

From the end of the war in Southeast Asia in 1975, until his death in 2004, Dellinger remained active as a writer and resister, particularly the effort to end the war in Iraq. In addition to editing and freelance writing, he supported initiatives for women's liberation and interracial justice and peace. An important topic of research for this good-natured grandfather and "one man revolution" was Vietnam, involving years of personal experience and study. Looking back at what he calls "mostly unknown history" prior to 1965 in *Vietnam Revisited*, he discusses U.S. policies "that had catastrophic results for millions of Vietnamese and hundreds of thousands of young Americans and their families, lovers, neighbors and friends." As a piece of investigative reporting, the book tells as much about the U.S. as it does about Vietnam, including the consequences, "if we fail to face up to these realities and change them."

Shortly after Dellinger's release from prison in 1945, in a concise, direct statement prompted by "the crowning infamy" of Hiroshima, Dellinger introduced a theme about American culture that he informed his later speeches and writings. He called for a campaign not only against militarism and conscription, but also against "an economic and social system that supports them." At the same time, he argued that such a "nonviolent war" must be uncompromising in its commitment to treat each person, "including the worst of our opponents, with all the respect and decency that he merits as a fellow human being." Only then will the effort be worthy of the ideals it seeks to serve.

106

In keeping with this earlier statement, Dellinger regarded U.S. nuclear war policy, in Vietnam and later Iraq, as logical expressions of a "profit-oriented economy and self-righteous foreign policy, both of which have been with us from the beginning." Although critical of a culture where "the health of the state conflicts with the health of the citizenry, and the prerogatives of property prevent the fulfillment of the people," Dellinger also acknowledged America's achievements, its promise, in charting and "imaging" the future.

Referring to Randolph Bourne's epigram, "War is the health of the State," then to William James's search for a "moral equivalent of war," Dellinger insisted that remaining aloof from justice struggles offered no politically effective substitute to war. Equally pointless is "a purist condemnation of those who, seeing no alternative," resort to armed struggle in resisting the institutionalized violence of slum, property, and money—in this country or other countries dominated by rich, imperial powers. The alternative, Dellinger said, is an international movement reflecting the needs and hopes of a diverse people, in campaigns committed to transforming conflict, without killing.

In a long and faithful commitment to the common good, he maintained a vision both utopian and practical about people's ability to choose for themselves without hurting one another. Respected for his intellectual honesty and integrity even by those who rejected his radical politics, he worked to build social order in which citizens "can do the things that fulfill them, in such a way that they express their dignity, their self-reliance, and their love for each other."

By David Dellinger

From Yale to Jail: The Life Story of a Moral Dissenter. New York: Pantheon, 1993.

Revolutionary Nonviolence: Essays. Indianapolis: Bobbs Merrill, 1970.

About David Dellinger

DeBenedetti, Charles, and Charles Chatfield. *An American Ordeal: The Anti-War Movement of the Vietnam Era.* Syracuse: Syracuse University Press, 1990.

The Power of the People. Active Nonviolence in the United States. Ed. Robert Cooney and Helen Michalowski. Philadelphia: New Society Publishers, 1987.

Muriel Rukeyser (1913-80)

She arrived in Worcester, Massachusetts, by bus from New York, in May 1974, where she was to give a poetry reading at the public library that very evening. The night before, she had attended a Broadway performance of *Ulysses in Nighttown*, a dramatization of the last section of Joyce's novel. Shortly after the bus pulled up to the curb, Muriel Rukeyser moved haltingly down the steps of the bus, looking as if' she had been jostled by a crowd of shoppers. Her hair, thin and graying, was in disarray; she wore dark fabric slippers, resembling ballet shoes, and her stockings sagged a bit below the black dress that hung unevenly just below the knees. Although she looked rather confused, she spoke the moment she recognized me, saying, "I haven't quite recovered yet from the play. The Molly Bloom soliloquy was so powerful— her story is every woman's story."

Two years later a friend of mine met her on a similar occasion. She told him that she had heard a woman (while pointing to her on the bus) say to her daughter, "Isn't that the worst looking woman you ever saw?"

Such memories remain, in part, because they conflict so decidedly with Muriel Rukeyser's appearance on stage, where she was a commanding, a noble presence. She read her remarkable poems in a clear, deep voice, in the grand manner, and the times I heard her she maintained complete command of the audience. There, as in private conversation, one was reminded of the young woman whose early photographs showed her to be strikingly beautiful, with large dark eyes, black hair styled in the 19th century manner, above a full, olive-colored face. She was conscious of her beauty, and the illnesses in later life and the increased weight troubled her and shook her confidence.

I think of her, aged 62, as she was photographed in 1975, in Seoul, Korea; she stood in the rain outside a prison, reading a statement on behalf of the poet Kim Chi Ha, a political prisoner under the military government there. Threatened with execution for his courageous defense of others, Kim Chi Ha is alive today partly as a result of Rukeyser's efforts, the support of Amnesty International and PEN. She had been involved in similar struggles ever since her journey to Alabama as a college sophomore in 1933 to cover the Scottsboro Boys Trial, when it was "illegal" to do so. And she spent time in jail in Manhattan and in Washington D.C., later, in support of draft resisters and in civil disobedience against the nuclear arms race. Even after two strokes in her mid-60s, prior to her death in February 1980, Rukeyser traveled and worked for social justice, particularly during her tenure as president of PEN, the international organization of poets, essayists, and novelists.

A member of a wealthy Philadelphia family, she was born in New York City on December 15, 1913, educated at experimental schools there and at Vassar College (with Mary McCarthy, Elizabeth Bishop, and Eleanor Clark). Shortly after leaving college she learned to fly a plane, and then turned to film editing, photography, traveling, and wrote for various periodicals. In 1935, she received the Yale Younger Poets Award for her first collection, *Theory of Flight*. Among her well-known early poems are "Boy with His Hair Cut Short," about a young man looking for work during the Depression, and "The Lynchings of Jesus" in which she said of the young black men, in the famous Scottsboro Boys Trial: "Dred Scott wrestles for freedom there in the corner/All our celebrated troubles are repeated here."

In 1936 she went to England and, eventually, to Spain to cover the People's Olympiad, an alternative to the Olympic Games being held in Berlin. The beginning of the Spanish Civil War gave her, as it gave George Orwell, a positive view of social change: "Even the gypsies on the docks in Barcelona were with this. It was a curious vision of a 20th century world which would not take place," she said later.

An assignment in the graphics division of the Office of War Information during World War II ended after only six months when, along with Ben Shahn and others, Rukeyser began to portray the deeper implications of the war. From there she moved to San Francisco, where she taught at the California Labor School, married, and gave birth to her only child, a son. At that time, she helped to initiate public poetry readings that contributed to the San Francisco Renaissance. Returning to New York in 1954, she taught at Sarah Lawrence College and was subsequently elected to the National Institute of Arts and Letters.

During the 1960s, Rukeyser gave benefit readings for the anti-war movement, and in 1972, she traveled on a peace mission to Hanoi with Denise Levertov and Jane Hart. The women's movement and two excellent films about her life and work gradually enlarged the audience for her poetry, even as failing health caused a curtailment of a busy schedule of readings, teaching, and writing in her last years.

Rukeyser's poetry reflects her strong sense of the common lot of ordinary people—their suffering, their work, their confusion in the midst of a sometimes cruel and awkward century. It is that consciousness of pain and her powerful rendering of that awareness that give her poetry its prophetic quality. Though written in some cases almost half a century ago, what she wrote seems especially current. The later poems, especially *The Speed of Darkness* (1968), about people out of work, about failures of communication between lovers, are **111** among the truly memorable lyrics of the period.

In her life and in her thirty books of fiction, poetry, and translations, Rukeyser was constantly striking out toward new territories. She did so not merely to rebel against convention, but in order to alert others to the peculiar tensions of the moment. This penchant for the unexpected kept her readers alert, and critics perpetually confused, so it will be some years before literary history and criticism attend to her achievements. In the meantime, the common reader, the one responsible for her present audience, keeps her work visible. I have never called her poems to the attention of readers and students without them responding with extraordinary enthusiasm.

Rukeyser was not a "thinker," and her writings sometimes sound rhetorical rather than analytical. Her language is the language of song. She seems not to speak to the immediate hurt or social concern, the way a more conventional writer would, but provides, one might say, something more essential: a psychological grounding for a private or political truth. One can only guess at the depth of suffering on her part that is at the base of such understanding. The strength at the heart of these insights is the reason, no doubt, that her poetry is both sustaining and lasting, as in "Poem":

> I lived in the first century of world wars.
> Most mornings I would be more or less insane,
> The newspapers would arrive with their careless stories,
> The news would pour out of various devices
> Interrupted by attempts to sell products to the unseen.
> I would call my friends on other devices;
> They would be more or less mad for similar reasons.
> Slowly I would get to pen and paper,
> Make my poems for others unseen and unborn.
> In the day I would be reminded of those men and women
> Brave, setting up signals across the vast distances,
> Considering a nameless way of living, of almost un-imagined values.
> As the lights darkened, as the lights of night brightened,
> We would try to imagine them, try to find each other.
> To construct peace, to make love, to reconcile
> Waking with sleeping, ourselves with each other.

Ourselves with ourselves. We would try by any means
To reach the limits of ourselves, to reach beyond
ourselves,
To let go the means, to wake.
I lived in the first century of these wars.

By Muriel Rukeyser

The Collected Poems. New York: McGraw Hill Co., 1978.

The Life of Poetry. New York: William Morrow and Co., (1949), 1974.

Interview. *The Craft of Poetry.* Ed. William Packard. Garden City, New York: Doubleday, 1974.

About Muriel Rukeyser

"How Shall We Tell Each Other of the Poet?" Ed. Anne F. Herzog and Janet Kaufman. New York: St. Martin's Press, 1999.

Kertesz, Louise. *The Poetic Vision of Muriel Rukeyser.* Baton Rouge: Louisiana State University Press, 1980.

Rosa Parks (1913-2005)

"Look, woman, I told you I wanted the seat. Are you going to stand up?"

"No."

"If you don't stand up, I'm going to have you arrested," the bus driver said.

"I'm not going to move."

Mrs. Rosa Parks had had a busy day at her job as a seamstress in a men's clothing store. Her neck and shoulder ached when she got on the bus. It was late afternoon, cold and dark, Montgomery, Alabama, December 1, 1955.

This episode involving Parks sometimes serves to introduce the story not of her life, but of a man who became very famous just after "she would not be moved." The dialogue repeated here, in fact, opens a biography of Martin Luther King, Jr., by David J. Carrow.

"I wasn't planning to be arrested at all," Parks admitted later. "I had a full weekend planned. It was December. Christmastime." As a tailor's assistant, she knew the next few weeks would be hectic, with a lot of sewing to do and alterations to make; also, as secretary of the Montgomery chapter of the National Association for the Advancement of Colored

People (NAACP), she "was preparing for the weekend workshop of the Youth Council," which she advised.

After James F. Blake, the bus driver, questioned her, policemen came onto the bus to warn Parks that, according to Alabama state law, she had to give up her seat to a white man. "Why do you treat us this way?" she asked. In refusing to stand, she helped to initiate a revolution that changed the South. Her arrest led the very next day to a boycott of the Montgomery buses by 50,000 black people, 75 percent of whom depended upon the public transit.

The boycott led, in turn, to local clergy forming the Montgomery Improvement Association and electing a young man named Martin Luther King, Jr., as its first chair. The twenty-six-year-old son and grandson of preachers and a doctoral candidate at Boston University's School of Theology, King had recently moved to the state capital of Alabama with his wife and young child. He had accepted a call as pastor of Dexter Avenue Baptist Church, a well-known black congregation in the shadow of the State Capitol Building.

The boycott of the buses following Parks' arrest lasted from December 1955 to December 1956, when the Supreme Court declared the law unconstitutional. At that point, Parks rode on a desegregated bus, again with driver James F. Blake. "He didn't react at all," she said later, "and neither did I."

Born February 4, 1913, in Tuskegee, Alabama, Rosa Louise McCauley was the daughter of James and Leona Edwards McCauley, a carpenter and teacher. When she was two, Rosa, her parents, and a younger brother moved to her grandparents' farm in the same state. She remembers "going to sleep as a girl hearing the Klan ride at night and hearing a lynching and being afraid the house would burn down." At eleven, she enrolled in a private industrial school for girls in Montgomery, which had been founded by white women from the North.

In 1932, Rosa McCauley married Raymond Parks, a barber, who had been working in voter registration campaigns and other civil rights causes for several years. Later she attended what is now Alabama State University, in **115** Montgomery, and worked with the Montgomery Voters

League, NAACP Youth Council, and other organizations. In 1943, Parks was elected secretary of the local branch of the NAACP; that same year, after she had paid her fare at the front, a bus driver had tried to make her leave the bus and enter again by the back door.

Although continually threatened and eventually fired from her job, Rosa Parks remained in Montgomery until 1957, a year after the successful bus boycott, when she and her husband moved to Detroit to live near her mother and brother. Her husband had suffered a breakdown in Alabama, and even though she continued fund-raising efforts for NAACP by appearing at rallies around the country, they endured several years of ill-health and low-paying jobs in Detroit. In 1965, John Conyers, Jr., a Michigan congressman and leader in civil rights, welfare, and anti-war movements, hired her to work in his office, where she met visitors and assisted him with various efforts on behalf of worker assistance. From then until her death forty years later, Rosa Parks remained active, a source of inspiration and commitment to people around the world.

In public appearances and occasional articles (particularly in connection with celebrations honoring the memory of Martin Luther King, Jr.), Parks was recognized for her essential contribution to a movement involving many talented and dedicated people. Her several projects for the common good included the Rosa and Raymond Parks Institute for Self-Development, initiated in 1987 (ten years after her husband's death), which focused on "the average child who may profit most from the lessons of history and from programs designed to foster awareness and involvement." One of its programs is the annual Reverse Freedom Tour, which takes teenagers on bus tours retracing the Underground Railroad, the route that 19th century slaves took to Canada, and visiting sites of the Civil Rights movement, including the spot where Parks "would not be moved."

Rosa Parks was not the first person arrested for refusing to "move to the back of the bus." A famous Supreme Court ruling against school segregation (Brown v. Board of Education of Topeka) in 1954 had given impetus to desegregation efforts in

116

Montgomery; and before Parks' arrest in 1955, when two young women had been arrested, campaigns had been organized around their trials. For various reasons, NAACP and the Women's Political Council, which had also been active on behalf of desegregation, decided not to pursue the cases in court. With Rosa Parks, they decided the time had come. Jo Ann Robinson, a woman active in the campaign, supported that decision because she regarded Parks as a person who could carry the weight of the case into court, someone who was "quiet, unassuming, and pleasant in manner and appearance; dignified and reserved; of high morals and strong character."

Mrs. Parks' husband felt differently. "The white folks will kill you, Rosa," he told her; others warned her as well. But thinking her appeal of the $14 fine might "mean something to Montgomery and do some good," Parks agreed to go along with the plan—and, of course, it did.

The story of Rosa Parks is powerful, in part because of her quiet courage and patience in accepting the risks associated with her arrest. Equally essential was the preparation she made for that moment in the years preceding it: the day-to-day, modest assignment and tedious hours as secretary of the NAACP; the educational outreach with the Youth Council; meetings with Myles Horton and Septima P. Clark at the Highlander Folk School, a Tennessee training institute for organizers; even—as she has suggested—her choice of a husband. (She knew of his work before their marriage in defense of the Scottsboro Boys, nine black youths unfairly convicted of raping a white woman in 1931.)

As a person and historical figure, Rosa Parks dramatized a fact evident in the history of nonviolent social change: the "ordinariness" of those responsible for momentous changes in human events—an "ordinariness" that is also extraordinary. An accident of history—the time, place, and person responsible for a turn of events—is almost never quite an accident, but a coming together of diverse and conscious forces. One person seizes the moment or several people nudge it toward the best possible conclusion. Gandhi did that, in initiating a famous **117** march to the sea, which in turn challenged British authority in

India and ended with India's independence; Ammon Hennacy and Dorothy Day did it, in encouraging nonviolent disobedience against civil defense drills, which in turn led to nuclear test ban treaties between the U.S. and the Soviet Union; Martin Luther King, Jr., did it, in recognizing Rosa Parks' contribution and learning as quickly as possible what Glenn Smiley and Bayard Rustin taught about orchestrating a large-scale nonviolent movement to end segregation in the South.

How often we relearn that social change comes not from one action or one person—though that one courageous act or astute person may "spark" a freedom movement, as the song, "Sister Rosa," says. Effective and lasting social change comes, ultimately—as the Civil Rights movement demonstrated—from action, cooperation, community that are sustained and carried on, often by "ordinary people" in "ordinary times."

By Rosa Parks

Rosa Parks: Mother to a Movement. New York: Dial Books, 1992.

About Rosa Parks

Branch. Taylor. *Parting the Waters: America in the King Years 1954-63.* New York: Simon and Schuster, 1988.

Carrow, David J. *Bearing the Cross: Martin Luther King, Jr., and the Southern Christian Leadership Conference.* New York: William Morrow and Co., 1986.

"Rosa Parks," *Current Biography Yearbook*, 1989, pp. 431-34.

Mulford Sibley (1912-1989)

Across four decades, in essays, books, and pamphlets, including *The Obligation to Disobey* (1970), Professor Sibley provided the most useful body of writings on the politics of pacifism since Gandhi. In the meantime, he maintained an active, even famous career as a teacher of political theory and as a civil libertarian and war resister.

Born in Marston, Missouri, on June 14, 1912, Mulford Q. Sibley grew up in Oklahoma, graduating from Central State University, Edmund, and the university in Norman in the mid-thirties; in 1938, he completed a doctorate in political science at the University of Minnesota. After teaching for ten years at the University of Illinois, he returned to Minneapolis/St. Paul, and taught at colleges and universities there, and throughout the United States and abroad. His other longtime associations include the American Service Committee and the Martin Luther King Institute of Nonviolent Social Change in Atlanta, which he advised.

In the Upper Midwest, Sibley is something of a legend as a teacher and Socialist. His debate with a St. Paul alderman in the late 1960s about who should or should not be allowed to espouse what causes on a state university campus attracted audiences throughout the region; it raised basic questions about the relationship between the university and the community among the general public, as well as among scholars and students throughout the United States.

The significance and originality of Sibley's political thought is best suggested by one of his earliest pamphlets, *The Political Theories of Modern Pacifism: An Analysis and Criticism* (1944), which contains both a summary of modern pacifist thought and a critique of its major arguments "insofar as they related themselves to the world of politics."

It describes the philosophical bases of Hindu pacifism, Christian pacifism, and the pacifism of the secular revolutionary movements of the 19th and 20th centuries, and then evaluates several main currents or propositions that all pacifist theories hold in common. Among them are: (1) that violence hinders the achievement of a democratic and peaceful order; (2) that decentralization in politics and in the economic order is desirable; and (3) that the ideology of nonviolence has a direct relevance to politics. The last two tenets provide modern pacifism with its greatest challenge, if, that is, it is to deal with questions that go beyond personal witness.

In showing how pacifism speaks to these concerns, Sibley prefers Gandhi's theory of politics to that of the Christian anarchists, secularists, or other utopians of the last two centuries, particularly regarding the State. "While the pacifist is right in protesting against the swallowing up of the individual personality by the Leviathan State," overemphasizing decentralization and agrarianism raises problems, too, he says. "A world in which the binding tie of political cohesion is practically severed would be a poor setting for social harmony and nonviolence."

Like Gandhi and unlike the anarchists, Sibley regards maintenance of the State as compatible with a pacifist ethic; and he argues against those, such as the late Reinhold Niebuhr, who say pacifism has no direct relevance to modern politics. It may, in fact, be "the only context in which to discover the road to a new polity," Sibley argues. "In this respect Hindu and secular revolutionary pacifism are far more penetrating than most emphases of Christian pacifism." Gandhi, for example, whose political theory involved a philosophy of history, as well as a theory of revolution, saw that in any mass action, previous agreement is essential "if the power of the State is to be effectively challenged."

It is against this background—providing a theoretical basis for a new politics based upon nonviolence—that Sibley's work is best understood, including his later discussions of power, authority, and violence. These concepts, as Hannah Arendt also has argued, must be clarified if one is to deal with the crucial issue in politics, Who rules whom?

In considering various sides of' this question, including those related to civil disobedience, Sibley calls upon a fund of knowledge of past nonviolent resistance—from his own book, *The Quiet Battle* (1968), as well as from the Civil Rights and anti-war movements and resistance to the nuclear arms race. He often supported an argument by reference to alternative or "revolutionary" practices, such as resisting conscription and war taxes, hiding political prisoners (Jews in Germany, for example, during World War II), and exposing secret government war agreements.

Sibley recognized at the same time the hazards that continue to make the application of the pacifist principles difficult "in a world that is more violent and less free" than it was previously. He wrote in *The Obligation to Disobey,*

> In attempting to make ends and means compatible with each other, the pacifist is both a revolutionary and a political realist. Only radical social reconstruction can provide a framework which will encourage respect for human personality. But peace cannot be attained by war, and reverence for human beings will not be advanced by methods deliberately meant to kill and maim them . . .

Only when radicals emancipate themselves from the fatal fascination which violence still apparently has for them can they become leaders in the cause of equalitarian revolution.

As political theory, the writings of Mulford Sibley deserve serious study by everyone who works for fundamental social change. As a scholar, teacher, and "quiet battler" in his own right, Sibley helped to lay the groundwork for a radical culture. In his own life, also, he provided a vivid example of the necessary relationship between political theory and practices between the politics of pacifism and nonviolent direct action.

Sibley was an especially popular teacher, admired even by those not particularly sympathetic to his pacifist and socialist politics. For forty years his tall, lanky figure was almost as much of an institution as the Mississippi River that cuts through the University of Minnesota campus, where he taught seminars on Plato and Marx, general courses in Medieval political thought and political theory, and served as adviser to the program in American Studies.

As a lecturer, Sibley was known for his ability to present all sides of a question fairly, even while making clear his own position. This reputation for integrity prompted several people, including a vice president of the United States, to come to his defense when political bureaucrats occasionally harassed him for questioning conventional behavior and publicly espousing unpopular causes.

By Mulford Sibley

The Obligation to Disobey: Conscience and the Law. New York: Council on Religion and International Affairs, 1970.

The Quiet Battle: Writings on the Theory and Practice of Non-violent Resistance. Garden City, N.Y.: Doubleday, 1963 and Boston: Beacon Press, 1968.

The Political Theories of Modern Pacifism: An Analysis and Criticism. Philadelphia: The Pacifist Research Bureau, 1944, 1970.

About Mulford Sibley

Morphew, Clark. "Peace Prof: Controversial Ideas Still Propel Mulford Q. Sibley." St. Paul (Minn.) *Post Dispatch* (March 3, 1984), pp. 1B-2B.

Helder Camara (1909-99)

You have a gun
And I am hungry
You have a gun
because
I am hungry
You have a gun
therefore
I am hungry

The speaker's tone of voice, in M.C. Acre's poem, is recognizably that of the late Dom Helder Camara. Native to one and formerly archbishop of another of the poorest, most "feudal" regions of Brazil, he recognized suffering resonant in the voices of landless peasants. Facts such as the following, involving millions of his people, shaped his ministry for forty years: $100 income per capita, 70 percent illiterate and with an infant mortality rate of 50 percent. Long before the Second Vatican Council led Latin American bishops at Medellin (1968) and Puebla (1979) to commit themselves to "a preferential option for the poor," Helder Camara had done so.

Faithfulness to the poor, a theme of his poetry and prose, **123** has inspired advocates for social justice throughout the world, and his work evoked awards and honorary degrees, as well as several nominations for the Nobel Prize. (In 1973, the year the Nobel Prize for Peace went to Henry Kissinger and Le Duc Tho, European workers, students, and others gave an "alternate" People's Peace Prize of $300,000 to Camara.) In organizing base communities and initiating the National Conference of Brazilian Bishops (CNBB) in 1952, he helped to reclaim a voice for the Brazilian church and its people. The Movement for Grassroots Education, another project, "developed over a thousand church-sponsored radio schools that brought poor people together in literacy circles in which they critically examined the region's poverty, malnutrition, and illiteracy." Penny Lernoux's *Cry of the People.* describes this movement's response to a repressive government, under a policy of "national security," that terrorized peasants, lay and clerical ministers associated with Christian renewal throughout Latin America.

Basic tools for Camara's educational movement were the Bible and the educational philosophy of his fellow Brazilian, Paulo Freire, in *Pedagogy of the Oppressed*. After a period of reform associated with that movement, Catholics influenced by it resisted the repression that followed a military coup in Brazil in 1964, the year Camara became archbishop of Recife. In that period, his life was threatened many times, his house machine-gunned, his name slandered, as the Brazilian media banned and blacklisted him for nine years. In a poem written about the same time, he described the basis of his commitment over the years.

> Hope without risk
> is not hope,
> which is believing
> in risky loving,
> trusting others
> in the dark,
> the blind leap....

124   Five feet four inches tall, weighing 120 pounds, Helder Pesoa Camara was often characterized as "frail," with an

energetic manner and an animated speaking style. Born February 7, 1909, in Fortaleza, on the northeastern coast of Brazil, he was one of thirteen children of a devout Catholic mother and a father who taught that "it is possible to be good without being religious." As a boy of fourteen, Camara entered the seminary nonetheless, was ordained in 1931, and spent the next five years as a priest in his native city. Attracted to the "Green Shirts," a Brazilian fascist party, because of its militant anti-communism, he said that his naivete at that time made it easier for him to understand others similarly misled.

Transferred to Rio de Janeiro in 1936, Camara gradually came to realize "the fallaciousness of the communism-anticommunism dichotomy." All around him were people ill and underfed, living in shacks and without hope. "They suffer the consequences of an extremism—a massive hysterical anticommunism," dramatizing the fact that "the most threatening clash of our time is not between East and West but rather between the developed and underdeveloped countries." Much of the suffering, represented by a high incidence of tuberculosis in his own region, arises from the rich maintaining their wealth while crushing their fellow citizens, he said. Injustices result, not just from "occasional events," but from structures, he said in 1977 in Washington, D.C., including corporations that cover the world and sometimes "ally themselves to military power and to governments."

Appointed auxiliary bishop of Rio de Janeiro in 1952, Camara founded the National Conference of Brazilian Bishops shortly afterward. Already, he was widely respected by lay and clerical leaders for his work in the slums and his sponsorship of cooperative apartments for poor families. During the Cold War, Camara criticized the super powers, "supreme examples of capitalism and socialism, [who] remain blind and deaf, enclosed and imprisoned in their egoism...Today 85 percent, tomorrow 90 percent, rot in misery in order to make possible the excessive comfort of 15 percent, tomorrow 10 percent of the world's population. Who cannot fail to understand the need for a structural revolution in the developed world?" he asked in **125** 1967.

As a participant in the Second Vatican Council, he announced that he was eager to see the church go boldly "in search of her lost poverty." Even during that Council, however, the Roman curia censored him when he suggested that the episcopate address social issues more directly. In response to their action, he circulated an open letter to his brothers at the Council urging them to forego privileges and decorative attire that scandalize and distance working-class Catholics from the clergy.

Named archbishop of Olinda and Recife by Paul VI (the same year that the military overthrew a reformist president in Brazil), Camara initiated the Action, Justice, and Peace Association to support a just wage among workers earning less than $350 a year. Addressing students at the Catholic University of Pernambuco, Brazil, the new archbishop spoke of his obligation, his right and duty, to sound such warnings, "to denounce whenever it is necessary, to stimulate, to question, to suggest, to discourage, to encourage," on the basis of the fact "that the fate of people is at stake, and they are our people, flesh of our flesh, blood of our blood."

As conditions worsened under a repressive government, Camara's close associate—and chaplain to the students at the University of Recife—was murdered; terrorists machine-gunned Camara's residence and terrorized other progressives in the city. After the death of Paul VI, the Roman curia moved against Camara once again, criticizing his leadership, including his associates and admirers, who included several liberation theologians and fellow bishops.

Throughout the campaign to discredit him, Camara insisted that the inspiration for his program for improving the lot of workers and peasants comes not from the writings of Karl Marx, but from papal encyclicals and Catholic social teaching. Or as a well-known poster of him says, "When I give food to the poor, they call me a saint. When I ask why the poor have no food, they call me a communist." During a meeting of fellow **126** clerics in Lima, Peru, he stood once in tears before other Latin American bishops, pleading with conservatives among them to stop playing into the hands of dictators by calling liberation theology "communist inspired." Influenced by the politics of greed, in the words of Alfred Kazin, members and supporters of the Reagan/Bush administrations repeated the same charge.

Michele Pellegrino, Archbishop of Turin, in his introduction to Camara's *The Church and Colonialism: The Betrayal of the Third World*, described his "frank and fervent word" as a worthy continuation of "the tradition of Basil, Ambrose, Chrysostom," early doctors of the church, and asked that it "arouse an uneasiness which may lead to a new search for the way of justice, love and peace." Although later replaced by a prelate less concerned about the issues that informed his predecessor's public ministry—Dom Helder Camara remains "a presence" in Brazil and wherever the church lives out its "preferential option for the poor." In his visits to the United States (and in an excellent film, *Excuse Me, America*, about Camara, Dorothy Day, and Cesar Chavez, at the 1978 Eucharistic Congress in Philadelphia), he called attention to suffering in this country that so frightfully resembles the consequences of injustice in his own.

In her poem, "Dom Helder Camara at the Nuclear Test Site," Denise Levertov conveys a vivid sense of his persistent, lively spirit in waging peace throughout his long life. After risking arrest in the Nevada desert, at a demonstration protesting weapons of mass destruction, "the "octarian wisp" joined others in a circle of celebration. "Light and persistent as tumbleweed,/but not adrift, Dom Helder,...faithful pilgrim, dances/dances at the turning core."

By Helder Camara

The Church and Colonialism:. The Betrayal of The Third World, Tr. William McSweeney. Denville, N.J.: Dimension Books, 1969.

The Desert Is Fertile. Tr. Dinah Livingstone. Maryknoll, N.Y.: Orbis Books, 1974.   **127**

About Helder Camara

De Broucker, Jose. *Dom Helder Camara: The Violence of a Peacemaker,* Tr. Herma Briiffault. Maryknoll, N.Y.: Orbis Books, 1970.

Hope, Marjorie, and James Young. *The Struggle for Humanity. Agents of Nonviolent Change in a Violent World.* Maryknoll, N.Y.: Orbis Books, 1977.

Lernoux, Penny. *Cry of the People: United States Involvement in the Rise of Fascism, Torture, and Murder and the Persecution of the Catholic Church in Latin America,* New York: Doubleday, 1980.

—. *People of God: The Struggle for World Catholicism.* New York: Viking Press, 1989.

Levertov, Denise, "Dom Helder Camara at the Nuclear Test Site," *Sands of the Well.* New York: New Directions, 1996, p. 114.

Franz Jagerstatter (1907-43)

Consider two things: from where, to where
Then your life will have its true meaning.

The Refusal, the title of the German film about his life, captures the spirit of the drama: an Austrian peasant's personal, but firm resistance to a despotic government. Although state and ecclesiastical authorities advised him to do as he was told, Franz Jagerstatter refused to support an unjust war. He suffered death rather than perform military service in Hitler's army.

Writing in a small composition book, in pencil, shortly before he was beheaded, he asked:

> For what purpose, then, did God endow all men with reason and free will if, in spite of this, we are obliged to render blind obedience; if, as many also say, the individual is not qualified to judge whether this war started by Germany is just or unjust? What purpose is served by the ability to distinguish between good and evil? I would be ready to exhibit unquestioning obedience, but only in circumstances where one would not be hurting others by doing so.

No one would be more surprised than Franz Jagarstatter at his present fame: not only from a well-known biography and several films, but also as a result of war resisters who regularly quote his journal in their applications for conscientious objection or in court, following arrests for civil disobedience against nuclear weapons. Recently, the president of Austria declared Jagerstatter a national hero; and authorities of the Roman Catholic church—in contrast to their wartime counterparts, who recommended that Jagerstatter ignore his conscience—are seriously considering his cause for canonization.

Born May 20, 1907, in St. Radegund, a small Austrian village near Bavaria, Franz Bachmeier was reared by his mother and stepfather. When his father was killed in the First World War, his stepfather, after marrying Franz's mother, adopted him, and later gave over his farm to him. Growing up, Franz Jagerstatter attended school in his home village, and as a young man gained a reputation for being robust, fun-loving, even rowdy.

In 1936, he married a woman from a village nearby; they went to Rome on their honeymoon. Born a Catholic, like everyone else in the village, Jagerstatter experienced a kind of religious conversion around this time, influenced perhaps by his devout wife. Over the next few years, when their three daughters were born, he became increasingly active in the small 15th-century parish church, where he served as sexton.

In 1938, when Hitler's army moved across the German border into Austria, Jagerstatter was apparently the only person in the village to vote against the take-over. His was a singular, personal resister, without any link to a political party or movement. Although he realized that clergy opposing the Anschluss might lose their religious freedom, he was discouraged by their voting for the National Socialists. The choice, he said later, was not much different from the one offered to the crowd on Maundy Thursday between "the innocent Savior and the criminal Barabbas." Gradually, Jagerstatter gave up arguing politics with his friends over beer—then cider—at the local inn, and responded to their greeting "Heil Hitler!" with "Pfui Hitler!"

130

Although he took part in some military training, Jagerstatter remained publicly anti-Nazi. When he was finally called to active duty in February 1943, he stuck with his plans, related earlier to his friends, to refuse to put on a uniform, even after they and the local priest told him it was folly to resist. His closest friend remembered saying "Go with God, Franz," the day he left the village, and his response, "You'll see no more of me."

A month later, while he was imprisoned at Linz, Jagerstatter wrote his wife that he had recently taken the difficult step of saying "No!" once again, and thanked her "for all the love and fidelity which you have brought me and the whole family. And for all the sacrifices you must still undergo for my account." At this time, the Bishop of Linz spelled out to Jagerstatter "the moral principles defining the degree of responsibility borne by citizens and private individuals for the acts of the civil authority."

Shortly afterward, Jagerstatter was transferred to a prison in Berlin, where he stood for a military trial on July 6, 1943. Sternly lectured by two high-ranking officials about his obligations to serve the Fatherland, he responded that he was well aware of the penalty, but he could not serve the regime.

Quotations from Jagerstatter's letters at this time reflect his obvious love for the countryside near his farm and his concern for conflicting obligations between his family and his conscience:

> Again and again people stress the obligations of conscience as they concern my wife and children. Yet I cannot believe that, just because one has a wife and children, he is free to offend God by lying (not to mention all the other things he would be called up to do). Did not Christ Himself say, "He who loves father, mother, or children more than Me is not deserving of my love?"

Though considered an enemy of the state, Jagerstatter appears to have been treated with consideration in prison, perhaps because of his sincerity, and the attorney appointed to defend him made an extraordinary effort to get him to recant. **131**

The lawyer arranged for Jagerstatter's pastor and wife to visit even after the trial, on July 15. About this time, he wrote, "These few words are being set down here as they come from my mind and my heart. And if I must write them with my hands in chains, I find that much better than if my will were in chains."

Several other Jagerstatter statements have great resonance for anyone concerned about the reluctance of private citizens, political and religious leaders to resist the rise of militarism and the nuclear threat since World War II. Almost as a challenge to what has been called "psychic numbing" (people's tolerance of nuclear destruction), Jagerstatter wrote, "One often hears it said these days that 'if it's all right for you to do this or that with an untroubled mind: the responsibility for what happens rests with someone else.' And in this way responsibility is passed on from one man to another. No one wants to accept responsibility for anything."

His last statements reflect as well the depth of his sanity and holiness, with numerous references to the basic truths of religious faith that seem ever radical, ever new: "The true Christian is to be recognized more in his works and deeds than in his speech. The surest mark of all is found in deeds showing love of neighbor.... Let us love our enemies, bless those who curse us, pray for those who persecute us. For love will conquer and will endure for all eternity."

Franz Jagerstatter was beheaded on August 9, 1943, and his ashes are buried in the churchyard in his native village. In a letter written only hours before his death, he promises his children, "I will surely beg the dear God, if I am permitted to enter heaven soon, that he may also set aside a little place in heaven for all of you.

In the village of St. Radegund, pilgrims make their way to his gravesite, particularly since the appearance of Gordon Zahn's biography, *In Solitary Witness: The Life and Death of Franz Jagerstatter* (1962). An American sociologist, Zahn is perhaps the most influential figure in the U.S. on Catholic social thought; he happened upon Jagerstatter's story almost by chance during research for an earlier book, *German Catholics and Hitler's War* (1962), a study of Catholic complicity with the Nazi government. Others credited with preserving Jagerstatter's remarkable story are two priests who knew him: his village pastor, who gathered letters, clippings, and notes about him, and a chaplain at the prison where he went to trial, who wrote articles about Jagerstatter following World War II.

Half a century after his death, these questions about the Austrian peasant, posed by Gordon Zahn, are still relevant: "The facts of Franz Jagerstatter's life may be stated briefly, but how does one begin to tell his real story? What was there about this man that, alone among his friends and neighbors, perhaps alone among all his Austrian co-religionists, made it possible for him to come to his fateful decision?" In an era prejudiced toward violence and killing, Jagerstatter's life remains as one of the most remarkable examples and gifts of nonviolent suffering and courage. How many lives might have been saved over 2000 years if Christians had refused to kill?

About Franz Jagerstatter

Zahn, Gordon C. "Clarifying the Disputed Witness of Franz Jagerstatter," *New Oxford Review*, September 1991, 14-19.

—. *German Catholics and Hitler's War*. Foreword by Daniel Berrigan. New York: E. P. Dutton and Co., 1969 (1962).

—. *In Solitary Witness: The Life and Death of Franz Jagerstatter*. Springfield, Ill.: Templegate, 1991 (1964).

Industrial Workers of the World (IWW)

> We condemn all wars, and for the preventions of such, we proclaim the anti-militarist propaganda in time of peace, thus promoting Class Solidarity among the workers of the entire world, and, in time of war, the General Strike in all industries.

Is it any wonder that workers who adopted this resolution at their convention in 1916 were eventually hounded, jailed, and exiled, once Woodrow Wilson involved the U.S. in the First World War. With one of their leaders in prison, they joined many others in a vigorous anti-war campaign, with their slogan, "Don't be a soldier, be a man. Join the I.W.W. and fight on the job for yourself and your class."

> With the European war for conquest and exploitation raging and destroying the lives, class consciousness and unity of the workers,...we openly declare ourselves the determined opponents of all nationalistic sectionalism, or patriotism, and the militarism preached and supported by our own enemy, the capitalist class.

134 Co-founded in Chicago in 1905, by William V. Haywood, Eugene Victor Debs, and Mother Jones, among others, the

Industrial Workers of the World ("Wobblies") committed themselves to radical actions and proselytizing in words and song. As Sidney Lens wrote, "Their lyrics had both the bite and the tang of America, eschewing all circumlocutions and vagaries," and satirized the American Federation of Labor as "the American Separation of Labor." Balladeers Ralph Chaplin and others wrote songs, substituting proletarian lyrics for old gospel hymns. Chapin's "Solidarity Forever" sang the praises of the unacknowledged builders of America:

It is we who plowed the prairies; built the cities where they trade;
Dug the mines and built the workshops; endless miles of railroad laid;
Now we stand, outcast and starving, 'mid the wonders we have made;
But the Union makes us strong.

Their most notable achievement was a victorious immigrant strike in Lawrence, Massachusetts, against the textile industry in 1912, where the average wage was sixteen cents an hour. During the nine-week struggle, police arrested 375 strikers, later released, and National Guard soldiers intervened to break the strike by falsely arresting two leaders, Joseph J. Ettor and Arturo Giovanitti, for murder. Through ingenuity and courage, the I.W.W. induced strikebreakers to quit, and eventually won the strike.

Secretary-treasurer of the Western Federation of Miners, before he co-founded the Wobblies and later took a leadership position, William V. (Big Bill) Haywood was born in Salt Lake City in 1869, and worked in the mines from the time he was fifteen. Defended by Clarence Darrow, Haywood was declared "not guilty" in a sensational murder trial in 1907, and played a central role in the Lawrence strike. Although Debs and the Socialist Party eventually dissociated themselves from the Wobblies, Debs continued to support their right to organize, but the I.W.W. eventually floundered from lack of organization, particularly after a defeat in the Paterson, New Jersey, 135 strike in 1913, and focused on organizing miners and foresters in the West. After entering World War I, the U.S. government, accused workers of disloyalty for opposing it, and succeeded crushed the labor movement, with particular vehemence toward the I.W.W. Haywood was prosecuted, and Debs eventually sent to federal prison, as were many members of the union, for draft and war resistance.

Although relatively short-lived, the achievement of the Industrial Workers of the World in the struggle for decent wages and working conditions was considerable at the time and significant in labor history. Among writers and artists of the early-20th century, including John Dos Passos, Dorothy Day, and editors of *The Masses*, their message and their commitment to workers were an inspiration. Organizing in areas where labor and living conditions were horrible, they employed new and imaginative strategies in their struggle, and are credited with early experiments with slow-down and sit-down strikes, which were employed successfully in the 1930s. Their efforts led to successful campaigns to unionize workers in forests and lumber camps in the Far West, and in oil fields of Kansas and Oklahoma.

For a variety of reasons, the Wobblies have enjoyed a fame quite beyond the size of their membership of about 100,000 members, which continues among recent activists in labor, civil rights, and peace movement. Among their best known members was the Wobblie balladeer, Joe Hillstron, who, as Joe Hill, has been celebrated by Utah Phillips and Joan Baez, in lyrics by Alfred Hayes and Earl Robinson:

> I dreamed I saw Joe Hill last night
> Alive as you and me.
> Says I, "but Joe, you're ten years dead."
> "I never died," says he.
>
> "Joe Hill ain't dead," he says to me.
> Joe Hill ain't never died.
> Where working men are out on strike."
> Joe Hill is at their side.

136   A Swedish immigrant and successful organizer among miners, he was arrested for murder, and was executed eventually by the State of Utah, on the basis of ambiguous evidence. The prosecution relied on the public conception of the I.W. W. as "a motley horde of hoboes...who will not work and whose philosophy is a philosophy simply of sabotage and the violent overthrow of 'capitalism'...they are arch-fiends and the dregs of society." Once the prosecution indicated that Hill was an I.W.W. agitator and the author of I.W.W. songs, conviction seemed inevitable. In an international campaign for his defense as he awaited execution, Elizabeth Gurley Flynn appealed to President Woodrow Wilson on Hill's behalf, but the Governor of Utah would not hear of it. The sentiment of Hill's last will and testament was, "Don't mourn. Organize." A telegram he sent to Big Bill Haywood in Chicago said, "It is only a hundred miles from here to Wyoming. Could you arrange to have my body hauled to the state line to be buried? I don't want to be found dead in Utah."

About the Industrial Workers of the World

Dubofsky, Melvyn. *We Shall Be All: A History of the IWW*. New York: Quadrangle, 1969.

Haywood, William D. *Bill Haywood's Book: The Autobiography of Big Bill Haywood*. New York: International Publishers, 1929.

Lens, Sidney, *Radicalism in America*. Rev. ed., Cambridge, MA: Schenkman Publishing Co., 1982.

Rebel Voices: An IWW Anthology. Ed. Joyce Kornbluh. Chicago: Charles H. Kerr, 1988.

George Orwell (1903-50)

As a young man, he called himself a Tory anarchist, indicating both his affection for English culture and his hatred of British imperialism. But by 1936, at 33, George Orwell identified himself as a Socialist. That was the political stance, in spite of his persistent criticism of fellow socialists, that he respected: the only one, he felt, that might resist the drift toward totalitarianism in England and in other liberal democracies after World War II. The danger lay in the structure imposed on any country preparing for total war with the Soviet Union, he told his publisher Fred Warburg, "and the new weapons, of which of course the atomic bomb is the most powerful and most publicized." It lay also "in the acceptance of a totalitarian outlook by intellectuals of all colours," and the corruption of language that accompanied it.

This drift—and the threat it posed to civil liberties—provided the theme for Orwell's last and most famous novel, *Nineteen Eighty-Four* (1949); but the political, social, and economic conditions leading up to that situation had been his concern for a long time, as early as *Homage to Catalonia* (1939), about the Spanish Civil War, and *Animal Farm* (1945), the brilliant Swiftian fable that became a best seller and later a popular film.

Contrary to popular opinion, *Nineteen Eighty-Four* (1949) is not about Stalinist Russia or Hitler's Germany, but about Great Britain and countries with similar forms of government, including the United States. It is a warning about what could happen to a democratic nation that centers all its energy and resources on war-making, on "right thinking," and on repressing points of view that conflict with the status quo. The novel ends with two powerful images of totalitarianism, one of "a boot stamping on a human face—forever," and another of Winston Smith's loving Big Brother. In the last scene, Smith smiles at the telescreen, "two gin-scented tears trickling down the side of his nose."

Orwell's warning may sound absurd to us who have survived the "real" 1984; and several critics have suggested that his prophecy was off the mark. But anyone who has paid attention to American history since 1945 will recognize those moments when American politics approached this absurdity.

During the 1950s, for example, militant anti-communism flourished under the leadership of Senator Joseph McCarthy and—with the complicity of Republicans and Democrats who should have known better—polluted the atmosphere. In such an atmosphere, as Orwell pointed out, everyone loses, especially those people so blinded by hatred and prejudice that they no longer know the difference between imaginary ills and real ones.

Under later administrations, the Orwell condition periodically recurred. Ronald Reagan, for example, described the Soviet Union as an "evil empire," and administrative statements about Latin America and about a "winnable" nuclear war resembled Big Brother's diatribes on the telescreen in *Nineteen Eighty-Four*. When this language was accompanied by censorship of the press, during the invasion of Grenada, Americans of every political persuasion—conservative, liberal, or radical—began to feel that basic democratic rights were endangered. From Thomas Paine to George Orwell, "common **139** sense" indicates that totalitarianism is best resisted not by labels, fear tactics, and belligerence, but by open and lively debate and freedom of information.

In *Nineteen Eighty-Four*, especially the epilogue on Newspeak, and in "Politics and the English Language," the most important essay on language in the 20th century, Orwell argued that cleaning up our language, making it more precise and concrete, improved our politics as well. He did this in his own writing through images—pictures and sensations—that left no doubt about the meaning of his argument. This was true when he focused on the injustices of his time or on the simple pleasures of everyday life: flowers in spring; strong, properly brewed tea; and the English countryside.

"Politics and the English Language," for example, which says that political language in our time "is designed to make lies sound truthful and murder respectable, and to give an appearance of solidity to pure wind," describes easily recognizable abuses of language from recent history.

> Defenseless villages are bombarded from the air, the inhabitants driven out into the countryside, the cattle machine-gunned, the huts set on fire with incendiary bullets; this is called "pacification." Millions of peasants arc robbed of their farms and sent trudging along the roads with no more than they can carry; this is called "transfer of population" or "rectification of frontiers."

"Such phraseology is needed," Orwell went on to say, "if one wants to name things without calling up mental pictures of them."

At a time when many of the ills that Orwell warned against still flourish, readers do well to return to the words and example of this just, rather witty, and very honest man. An unsparing critic of all undemocratic practices, he once described his reason for writing in this way: "Every line of serious work I have written since 1936 has been written directly and indirectly against totalitarianism and for democratic socialism." A writer of astonishing integrity, he held to that position, through years of neglect, poverty, and three final years of illness, while completing *Nineteen Eighty-Four*.

Ammon Hennacy   Wilfred Owen

Bertrand Russell   George Orwell

141

Born Eric Arthur Blair, in Motlhari, Bengal (Burma), on June 25, 1903, "George Orwell" moved back to England as a child with his mother just before his father retired from the Indian Civil Service. Orwell attended two prestigious schools on scholarship, St. Cyprian's, which he described in "Such, Such Were the Joys," and Eton. Rather than go on to the university, he joined the Imperial Indian Police in 1922, and served in various posts in Burma until 1927. Reconciled to becoming a writer, he spent much of the next two years in Paris in rather severe poverty, as a dishwasher, tutor, and teacher. This experience and two years living among tramps in England provided material for *Down and Out in Paris and London* (1933). Subsequently, he taught "at one of the most godforsaken places I have ever struck," and worked in a bookshop, while he wrote two novels and an account of working-class life in England. After his marriage to Eileen O'Shaughnessy in 1936, he went to fight on the Republican side against Franco, in the Spanish Civil War. Wounded and ill from tuberculosis, he lived in Morocco for a year.

Physically unfit for service in the army during World War II, Orwell joined the Local Defense Volunteers, worked for the BBC, and wrote for a Socialist weekly as literary editor. The publication of *Animal Farm* in 1945, the year of his wife's death, made him famous on both sides of the Atlantic. No longer financially dependent on jobs as a journalist, he moved to the island of Jura, in Scotland; there, in declining health, he completed his last novel, *Nineteen Eighty-Four*. Returning to a sanitorium in England and, later, a hospital in London, he married Sonia Brownell in October 1949 and died three months later, on January 21, 1950. He remains perhaps the most essential writer of our time.

Orwell's best epitaph is in "Why I Write," about his wish to make political writing into an art:

> My starting point is always a feeling of partisanship, a sense of injustice. . . . But I could not do the work of writing a book, or even a long magazine article, if it were not also an aesthetic experience. So long as I remain alive and well I shall continue to take pleasure in solid objects

and scraps of useless information. It is no use trying to suppress that side of myself. The job is to reconcile my ingrained likes and dislikes with the essentially public, non-individual activities that this age forces on all of us.

By George Orwell

The Collected Essays, Journalism, and Letters of George Orwell, 4 vols. Ed. Sonia Orwell and Ian Angus. New York: Harcourt, Brace, and World, 1968.

Animal Farm. New York: Harcourt, Brace, 1954.

Homage to Catolonia. New York: Harcourt, Brace, and World, 1952.

Nineteen Eighty-Four, A Novel. New York: Harcourt, Brace, 1949.

Down and Out in Paris and London. New York: Harcourt, Brace, and World, 1933.

About George Orwell

Crick, Bernard R. *George Orwell: A Life.* Boston: Little, Brown, 1980.

George Orwell: A Collection of Critical Essays. Ed. Raymond Williams. Englewood Cliffs, New Jersey: Prentice Hall, 1974.

Woodcock, George. *The Crystal Spirit: A Study of George Orwell.* Boston: Little, Brown, 1966.

The World of George Orwell. Ed. by Miriam Gross. New York: Simon and Schuster, 1973.

Dorothy Day (1897-1980)

Dorothy Day is a model for our times for several reasons. First, because she was peculiarly, deeply, and undeniably American, and thus brought a very special character to her life as a Christian. Although she loved Russian, French, British, and Italian novelists—particularly Dostoevsky, George Bernanos, Dickens, Qrwell, and Ignazio Silone—she was a child of the American experience, and her religious commitment and vocation were bound up with this country. Her early family life, which was casually religious, her formal education in public schools and at the University of Illinois, as well as her admiration for William James's Varieties of Religious Experience, shaped her sensibility. She was a disciple of the American radical tradition, persistently anarchist and religious, from Thomas Paine to Martin Luther King, Jr. Her close association with The Masses, Mike Gold, and Ammon Hennacy—as well as her admiration for Eugene Victor Debs, Emma Goldman, and Elizabeth Gurley Flynn—was formative and enduring. Peter Maurin, a French peasant, was her teacher once she became a Catholic; but her temper was in the American grain.

Second, because she was a member of the laity. Unlike many religious figures held up for imitation to young people, she was not a cleric. She belonged to that group that emerged as a shaping force in the church at the time of the Second Vatican Council. As a 20th century heroine who faced the anxieties and challenges of a violent century, she was not so far removed from us as to appear foreign or aloof.

Third, because she failed, like most people, at many things—as a wife, in an early marriage, and perhaps as a parent. Although many of us see Dorothy Day as triumphant, as a success, one must acknowledge also her judgment of her life in *The Long Loneliness* (1952): "I feel that I have done nothing well. But I have done what I could." She often said that she took on certain responsibilities only because others (Peter Maurin, Ammon Hennacy, Karl Meyer) pushed them upon her. Although faithful and resilient, she never pretended to be all-knowing or all-powerful.

> Sometimes the only thing that keeps a woman going is the necessity of taking care of her young. She cannot sink into lethargy and despair because the young ones are dragging at her skirts, clamoring for something—food, clothing, shelter, occupation. She is carried outside herself.

Fourth, because she was a writer, the kind of writer that the language needs at this moment. She understood the power of everyday speech, and wrote in a manner that was understandable to everyone. Although she had a complex and demanding message to communicate, she fashioned a style that shunned pretension, artifice, or "rhetoric" in order to convey that message. On the works of mercy, she wrote, for example: "Martyrdom is not gallantly standing before a firing squad. Usually it is the losing of a job because of not taking a loyalty oath or buying a war bond, or paying a tax. Martyrdom is small, hidden, misunderstood." Elsewhere, in a meditation on the virtue of obedience, she said:

> Obedience is a matter of love, which makes it voluntary, not compelled by fear or force. Pope John's motto was "Obedience and Peace." Yet he was the pope who flouted

conventions which had hardened into laws as to what a pope could and could not do, and the Pharisees were scandalized and the people delighted.

Fifth, because she internalized values associated with peace and justice and gave them substance. In her devotion to voluntary poverty, to nonviolence, and to the radical reconstruction of the social order, she lived among workers, radicals, prisoners, and the down and out. For Christians, she came as a great shock. Here, in the life and vocation of one woman were the values that had been held up to church members, but often by people who did not embody them. Through her, the words became flesh: devotion to the poor, resistance to war, vulnerability toward circumstance, and charity to everyone.

Born in Brooklyn, on November 8, 1897, Dorothy Day lived briefly in San Francisco, but grew up in Chicago, where her father worked as a journalist. At 15, she won a scholarship to the University of Illinois and there became a socialist. Two years later, she returned to New York City, where she lived most of her life. As a young radical, she was arrested with the Wobblies (Industrial Workers of the World) and the suffragettes, as she was later with war resisters and United Farm Workers. During World War I, she wrote for *The Masses* and during the 20s lived in Greenwich Village, where she became friends with Eugene O'Neill, Malcolm and Peggy Cowley, Allen Tate, Caroline Gordon, and Kenneth Burke. At that time, she worked as a nurse, wrote a novel, *The Eleventh Virgin*, married, and lived briefly in Mexico.

In 1926, Day's conversion to Catholicism led to her separation from her second husband, Foster Batterham, and to a break with some of her radical friends. During those years, she supported herself and her only daughter, Tamar Teresa, by writing for *America, Commonweal*, and other periodicals.

On May 1, 1933, five months after meeting Peter Maurin, Dorothy Day founded the *Catholic Worker*, a monthly newspaper dedicated to making known "the expressed and implied teachings of Christ." It is published today, as it was over fifty years ago, at a penny a copy, with a circulation of 100,000. In the years between 1933 and her death in December

146

1980, Dorothy Day lived at various Houses of Hospitality and Catholic Worker farms near New York City, edited the newspaper, wrote five books, and spoke frequently at colleges, universities, churches and Catholic Worker communities throughout the United States.

Over those decades, she emerged as the most remarkable person in the history of American Catholicism and in some ways the most influential. Although few people managed, like her, to make a total commitment to voluntary poverty, personalism, or Christian anarchism, they often learned a great deal from her, and some went on to significant vocations modeled on her example.

Through her work—feeding the poor and housing the homeless, through her newspaper and her monthly column, "On Pilgrimage," and through her war tax resistance and civil disobedience, Dorothy Day touched the lives of numerous people: workers, intellectuals, students, clergy, and women of' three generations. Among the writers and editors who, at various times, helped to edit the *Catholic Worker* are Michael Harrington, author of *The Other America*; John Cogley, James O'Gara, and John Cort, editors of *Commonweal*; Tom Cornell and James Forest, co-founders of the Catholic Peace Fellowship; Jack Cook, author of *Rags of Time: A Season in Prison*: as well as a host of other artists and radicals who contributed to its pages: Ammon Hennacy, W.H. Auden, Gordon Zahn, Ade Bethume, Thomas Merton, Daniel Berrigan, Philip Berrigan, Eileen Egan, Fritz Eichenberg, Rita Corbin.

When Dorothy Day died, December 1980, she was mourned by the down-and-out in Manhattan, whom she fed and clothed, as well as by the great and famous, including the cardinal archbishop of New York, who came to bless her coffin. Many regard her as a saint.

By Dorothy Day

By Little and By Little: The Selected Writings of Dorothy Day. Ed. **147** Robert Ellsberg. New York: Alfred A. Knopf, 1983.

The Dorothy Day Book: A Selection from Her Writings and Readings. Ed. Margaret Quigley and Michael Garvey. Springfield, Illinois: Templegate Press, 1982.

On Pilgrimage: The Sixties. New York: Curtis Books, 1972.

Loaves and Fishes. New York: Harper and Row, 1963. 1983.

The Long Loneliness: An Autobiography. New York: Harper and Row, 1952 (1982).

About Dorothy Day

Coles, Robert and Jon Erikson. *A Spectacle Unto the World: The Catholic Worker Movement.* New York: Viking, 1973.

Miller, William D. *A Harsh and Dreadful Love: Dorothy Day and the Catholic Worker Movement.* New York: Liveright, 1973.

Piehl, Mel. *Breaking Bread: The Catholic Worker and the Origin of Catholic Radicalism in America.* Philadelphia: Temple University Press.

Ammon Hennacy (1893-1970)

Ammon Hennacy was arrested thirty-two times during his lifetime for various acts of civil disobedience—in Omaha, in New York City, and in his native Ohio (during the First World War). From 1918 to 1922, he did time for draft resistance, in Atlanta Federal Prison, where Eugene Victor Debs and Alexander Berkman, Emma Goldman's lover, were confined about the same time. After his release from that prison, Ammon and his common-law wife, Selma, walked across much of the United States and climbed Pike's Peak, in Colorado. That activity was a kind of therapy, Dorothy Day said, after the hard times in solitary confinement. Ammon had been placed in solitary after leading a strike against conditions in the jail, when he learned that the guards dined on food meant for the inmates while serving spoiled fish to the prisoners.

Ammon said that his moral education began with that imprisonment, although he had previously showed extraordinary courage in standing against conscription during World War I. One of the most moving passages in his autobiography, *The Book of Ammon* (1965), describes his journey out of despair, and gradual conversion to Christian nonviolence:

I had passed through the idea of killing myself. This was
an escape, not any solution to life. The remainder of my
two years in solitary must result in a clear-cut plan
whereby I could go forth and be a force in the world. . .
.Gradually I came to gain a glimpse of what Jesus meant
when he said that the Kingdom of God must be in
everyone: in the deputy, the warden, in the rat, and the
pervert. To change the world by bullets or ballots was a
useless procedure. . . . Therefore the only revolution
worthwhile was the one man revolution within the heart.
Each one would make this by himself and not need to wait
on a majority.

Born in Negley, Ohio, on July 24, 1893, Ammon Hennacy
joined the Ohio Socialist Party and the Industrial Workers of
the World (the Wobblies) at sixteen. After a year at Hiram
College, he went to the University of Wisconsin, where he once
gave up his bed to Randolph Bourne, the social and literary
critic who had come to speak in Madison in 1914. From there
Ammon returned to Ohio State University for a year and then
to full-time organizing for the party of Eugene Victor Debs and
for resistance to the draft. Following the prison term in Atlanta,
he visited radical communes, farmed in Wisconsin, and wrote
for various radical periodicals, including *Mother Earth*, founded
earlier by Emma Goldman.

As a social worker in Milwaukee in the 1930s, he lived
with his wife Selma and two daughters, Carmen and Sharon.
After 1937, when he met Dorothy Day, he became a contributor
to the *Catholic Worker*. Their first meeting, important to both of
them, is described early on in his autobiography:

Dorothy Day spoke at the Social Action Congress in
Milwaukee, being invited there by Bishop (later Cardinal)
Strich. . . . In answering questions from patriotic
questioners she mentioned something of my pacifist
record, saying that I was not a Catholic, but an anarchist
and that when the next war came she would be with me in
opposition to it. Her continued refusal to follow the party
line of most churchmen in praising Franco gained my
admiration.

The uncompromised principles and the practical wisdom, the idea and the deed, appear side by side in *The Book of Ammon*, as well as in his posthumously published *The One Man Revolution in America* (1970), a collection of portraits and quotations of eighteen great Americans, from, John Woolman, Thomas Paine, and Thomas Jefferson (the only president in the group), to Dorothy Day and Malcolm X. As an anarchist Ammon would not allow his two books to be published commercially; that meant earning money for the tax collection and, therefore, for warmakers. These extraordinary works, privately printed, are now available from his widow (Joan Thomas, P.O. Box 25, Phoenix, Arizona 85001). Although casual in style and organization, they belong in every public library and peace education center.

Ammon Hennacy was, I think, the most courageous man I have ever known, in his insistence on speaking truth to power and in resisting injustice. Being with him or hearing him lecture—on a street corner, on a talk show, or in an auditorium, one felt as if he had suddenly caught the pulse of the American radical tradition. Even at 70, Ammon's face was animated and friendly, although lined from years spent laboring in the fields, on the picket line, and in prison.

It would be ridiculous, however, to romanticize Ammon Hennacy. He could be contentious, cantankerous, and stubborn, often confronting his listener with theories on nutrition ("no fish, flesh, or fowl") or his favorite sayings on diverse subjects. He advised reading the morning newspaper "to find out what the bastards are up to today." Persistent in his radicalism and repetitious in his teaching, he brought many people into movements for social change by selling the *Catholic Worker* on the street corner, and by his own example. Dorothy Day, who said Ammon's books resembled Thoreau's, but with a sense of humor, admitted that he had challenged her into taking a stand on issues that she might otherwise have neglected.

In the 1960s, Ammon opened a Catholic Worker House for ex-prisoners and others on the road in Salt Lake City. It was **151** named for Joe Hill, the Wobblie organizer and balladeer who was killed by the state of Utah in 1915. (Utah Phillips and Joan Baez sing the famous song immortalizing him: "I dreamed I saw Joe Hill last night/alive as he could be.") Ammon took a grocery cart to nearby supermarkets each morning to beg food—day old bread and vegetables for the soup line at his House of Hospitality. Each year, even while picketing daily against capital punishment, he fasted one day for each year since 1945 when the atomic bomb fell on Hiroshima and Nagasaki.

He was a crusty old Irishman with a marvelous capacity for talk and a love of poetry, especially William Blake and Edwin Markham. Many people, in fact, found him too gregarious. Like Peter Maurin, the co-founder of the Catholic Worker movement, Ammon never tired of preaching the gospel of Christian anarchism. Though critical of anyone who "chickened out" in the struggle for peace, he was also kind and generous, and able to appreciate the best in people who disagreed with him (and most people did).

Ammon's numerous actions in the nonviolent tradition included protests against capital punishment and against mock atomic-air-raid drills in Manhattan in the 1950s. His last leaflet, with the heading "Thou Shalt Not Kill," was distributed on the picket line in front of the state capitol building in Salt Lake City shortly before he died in January 1970. Among the many statements for which he is remembered is this bit of wisdom, written after a day in the fields, in 1945:

> Love without courage and wisdom is sentimentality, as with the ordinary church member. Courage without love and wisdom is foolhardiness, as with the ordinary soldier. Wisdom without love and courage is cowardice, as with the ordinary intellectual. Therefore, one who has love, courage, and wisdom is one in a million, who moves the world, as with Jesus, Buddha, and Gandhi.

By Ammon Hennacy

The One Man Revolution in America. Salt Lake City: Ammon Hennacy Publications, 1970.

The Book of Ammon, originally published as *Autobiography of a Catholic Anarchist.* New York: Catholic Worker Books, 1954.

About Ammon Hennacy

Day, Dorothy. "Picture of a Prophet." *Loaves and Fishes.* New York: Harper and Row, 1963.

Piehl, Mel. *Breaking Bread: The Catholic Worker and the Origin of Catholic Radicalism in America.* Philadelphia: Temple University Press, 1982.

Wilfred Owen (1893-1918)

Everyone, Gandhi said, must have a text to examine, to compare, and to test his or her life against. For this purpose, the writings of recent poets and artists have been especially valuable sources of inspiration and wisdom for people working in social justice. During the Vietnam and Iraq wars, this was especially true for the writings of Wilfred Owens, a young poet who died in the First World War and whose poems provided the text for Benjamin Britten's *War Requiem* (1963).

Among modern writers, no one understood and revealed the philosophical and religious implications of modern warfare better than Wilfred Owen, writing from the Western Front, 1916-18. In his letters and poems, he struggled with the basic conflict between his life as a soldier and the commandment to love his neighbor, between his hatred of the war and his dedication to solders under his command.

In Owen's writings, "the language of the Bible rises like water in the well of his subconscious mind, polluted by war, like the ravaged countryside where he fought and died," according to his biographer, Jon Stallworthy. Owen's letter to a friend in June 1918, for example, spoke in this way of having drilled his troops with helmets and rifles the day before:

For 14 hours yesterday I was at work—teaching Christ to lift his cross by numbers, and how to adjust his crown; and not to imagine thirst till after the last halt. I attended his supper to see that there were no complaints, and inspected his feet to see that they would be worthy of the nails. I see to it that he is dumb and stands to attention before his accusers. With a piece of silver I buy him every day, and with maps I make him familiar with the topography of Golgotha.

The passage is characteristic one, like so many of his poems, that is self-accusing without self-pity. In it, Owen indicates a sound awareness of how, as an officer in charge of troops, he could not extricate himself from the barbarous task of war. By his acts, he implicated himself as surely as Pilate's soldiers or Caesar's armies involved themselves in the death of Christ at Golgotha, "the place of the skull." Owen speaks not of hereditary or generalized guilt, but of his personal responsibility for actions on the side of death.

Wilfred Owen was, at the time of this letter to Osbert Sitwell, twenty-five years old. The oldest child of a lower middle-class family, he was born in Ostwestry, England, on March 18, 1893, and attended grammar schools in Birkenhead and Shrewsbury, but did not qualify for a university scholarship.

He educated himself, nonetheless, through courses at the university college in Reading, an hour west of London, and through work as a tutor in England and France before the war. Those years included time as a lay assistant at the vicarage of Reverend Herbert Wigan, in Dunsden. At nineteen, Owen thought seriously of becoming an Episcopal priest himself, but went through a religious crisis prompted by a disillusionment with conventional Christianity. About the same time, he rediscovered the poems of John Keats, and once in the army rapidly matured as a poet.

Wounded in 1917, probably suffering from shell-shock, he spent time in Craiglockhart Hospital, near Edinburgh. There he met Siegfried Sassoon, a published poet, who encouraged him. **155** Eventually Owen published a few lyrics in leading periodicals, powerful poems suggesting an acute modern sensibility, revolutionary for the time. By June 1918, he felt a responsibility to return to the Western Front, in northern France. On November 4 of that year, one week before the Armistice, after successfully leading his troops across a canal near Ors, he was killed. Although Owen left only a small body of work, his posthumously collected poems are generally regarded as some of the masterworks of modern literature and, indeed, in the canon of English poetry.

A good example of this achievement is "Futility," written about the same time as the prose statement quoted above. The speaker in the poem is a soldier who stands above the body of his dead comrade, asking, in despair: "Was it for this the clay grew tall?" Dazed, the speaker wonders why the sun, that once brought life and stars out of the cold earth, is now powerless to raise his comrade from the dead?

> Move him into the sun –
> Gently its touch awoke him once,
> At home, whispering of fields unsown.
> Always it woke him, even in France.
> Until this morning and this snow.
> If anything might rouse him now
> The kind old sun will know.
> Think how it wakes the seeds,—
> Woke, once, the clays of a cold star.
> Are limbs, so dear achieved, are sides,
> Full-nerved—still warm—too hard to stir?
> Was it for this the clay grew tall?
> —O what made fatuous sunbeams toil
> To break earth's sleep at all?

The questions in the second stanza are posed to no one in particular, yet the implication remains that God, in a sense, is on trial. Why did He bother creating the earth if—in the end—a young man at the height of his powers, in strength, beauty, and intelligence, must die so meaninglessly? Why did He make the sun so powerful, if it cannot—in all its glory—raise this young man, the end point of a diverse and complicated evolutionary process, to life?

The questions posed by Owen's poems seem almost instinctive. How can anyone, particularly a religious person, he asks, stand casually by while the forces of death triumph all around? Such provocative questions with psychological and political as well as religious implications suggest at least two reasons for the continuing importance of his work: (1) Owen understood the significance of the First World War, in that it would profoundly alter the nature of religious belief, destroying the past or rendering it useless for many people. Human beings, in discovering the scale of destruction possible in mechanized warfare, were literally unhinged by that awareness, as Ernest Hemingway and T.S. Eliot would indicate in stories and poems of the 1920s; (2) Owen understood also how he, as an actor in history, was responsible for war's destruction, preparing his men, his other Christs, for the crown of thorns. He recognized that even with the best intentions, people capitulate to the forces of death, out of conformity, laziness, moral indifference.

Such cooperation with death eventually undermines not only a person's belief, but also the nature of the church, Owen said to his mother, in a 1917 letter.

> Already I have comprehended a light which never will filter into the dogma of any national church; namely, one of Christ's essential commands was. . . be bullied, be outraged, be killed; but do not kill. It may be chimerical and an ignominious principle, but there it is. It can only be ignored, and I think pulpit professionals are ignoring it very skillfully.

In the same letter, Owen complained, "The practice of selective ignorance is one cause of war. Christians have deliberately cut some of the main teachings of their code."

For Owen, the main teaching that had been cut was Christ's disavowal of killing, and anyone trying to live as a Christian in this century is likely to be rather shocked by Owen's pointed remark. In his poems, also, he gave a realistic view of warfare, after the idealized view projected by the 157 Romantic and Victorian traditions. His anti-war sentiments, in fact, resembled those of Leo Tolstoy's pamphlets on Christian tradition of nonviolence thirty years before. Coincidentally, during the early days of the war, Owen lived in the home of a French poet influenced by Tolstoy's writings, and sent home drawings of wounded soldiers brought by train to the south of France.

Out of the depth of his imagination, Owen dramatized the threat to life rendered by modern warfare. In ironic poems such as "Dulce Et Decorum Est" and "Insensibility," he asked conventional believers to recognize their failure to uphold the teachings of Jesus and thereby focused attention on a major dilemma for contemporary Christians.

Simone Weil's statement, during the Second World War, that the distance separating the individual or the church from the essential Christian message of peace results in a painful spiritual state. In his poems and letters, Wilfred Owen arrived at a similar truth thirty years before. It is one that must be recognized, he thought, if the ethics of Christianity are ever to inform people's lives and actions. This is especially true in an age when everyone, as Owen said, lives on an extended battle-field and where, in a nuclear age, "Christ dies daily in No Man's Land."

By Wilfred Owen

Wilfred Owen: War Poems and Others. Ed. Dominic Hibberd. London: Chatto and Windus, 1975.

The Poems of Wilfred Owen. Ed. Jon Stallworthy. New York: W.W. Norton, 1986.

About Wilfred Owen

Hibberd, Dominic. *Wilfred Owen. British Council Pamphlet*. London: Longman Group Ltd., 1975.

Stallworthy, Jon. *Wilfred Owen: A Biography*. New York: Oxford University Press, 1974.

Elizabeth Gurley Flynn (1890-1964)

Ammon Hennacy, American anarchist and Catholic worker, admired people, as he said, "who never chickened." Among those whom he praised for her consistency and courage was Elizabeth Gurley Flynn, whose life was dedicated to gaining rights for and improving conditions of workers. With Eugene Victor Debs and Emma Goldman, Flynn is one of the great radicals of the early 20th century, who suffered for her persistence: loss of her husband and a lover, dismissal from the civil liberties organization she co-founded, and—at sixty—imprisonment.

As a young woman Flynn, like Abby Kelley Foster, was famous for her beauty; with her clear voice and golden-red hair, she was a striking presence on the lecture platform and the picket line. In a memoir at the time of Flynn's death, Dorothy Day recalled the young rebel's effect on a crowd:

> She charmed us out of our meager money; people emptied their pockets when the collection was taken for the strikers. I forsook all prudence and emptied my purse, not even leaving myself carfare to get back to the office. . . .In this way she aided countless workers—miners through

the far West, workers in wheat, lumber, textiles, all have benefited from her early work.

Flynn gave her first speech for socialism at 16, in 1906, in the Bronx, with the encouragement of her parents and to the delight of reporters for the New York newspapers. From then until her death at seventy-four, she was the subject of articles detailing her defense of Wobblies in the Pacific Northwest and the Mesabi Iron Range; her stormy love affair with Carlo Tresca, the hero of the Lawrence, Massachusetts, strike in 1912; and other labor and civil liberties disputes. To her many other causes she added, during her last years, that of prison reform; and *My Life as a Political Prisoner* (1963), about her twenty-eight months in Alderson (W. Va.) Federal Reformatory, is a powerful indictment of the system.

Born in Concord, New Hampshire, on August 7, 1890, Elizabeth Gurley Flynn grew up in the Bronx, where her mother insisted they settle in 1900. Her father, a ne'er-do-well, whom Elizabeth later accused of hiding behind her "radicalism" as an excuse for not holding a job, encouraged her interest in socialism. She read widely in the utopian novels and tracts of Mary Wollstonecraft, Edward Bellamy, and William Morris, and in her youth admired the anarchists Emma Goldman and Alexander Berkman, whom she met and followed. She joined the Industrial Workers of the World during its first year, in 1906, and two years later married John Archibald Jones, a miner active in the I.W.W. She had two sons by Jones, one of whom died in infancy; the second, reared principally by Elizabeth's mother and sister, died in 1940. After divorcing Jones, who expected her to give up organizing and agitation, Elizabeth Gurley fell in love with Carlo Tresca, a handsome Italian anarchist. Although they separated about 1930, she mourned him for many years after his death in 1943.

Victimized by various laws harassing radicals, particularly during the Red Scare following World War 1, Flynn combined labor organizing and legal defense for workers. From 1926 to 1930, she chaired the International Labor Defense, many of whose members were affiliated with the Communist party;

in 1930, she herself joined the party. In 1940, the American Civil Liberties Union, which she had helped to establish, expelled her from its executive board because of her communist affiliations, a decision rescinded only after her death.

In the second Red Scare, after World War II, Flynn was indicted for advocating the overthrow of the government. Hers was a typical political arrest during the McCarthy days:

> On a hot morning in June, 1951, the bell of our apartment on East 12th Street in New York City rang insistently. A knock came on the door, too soon for anyone to have climbed the three flights of stairs after we had pressed the button to open the downstairs door.
>
> Three F.B.I. agents, two men and a woman, roughly pushed their way past [my sister]. They stated they had a warrant for my arrest. I took the document and read it. It was for alleged violation of the infamous Smith Act. "For teaching and advocating the violent overthrow of the government, when and if circumstances permit," it said.

With several old associates, some crippled with age, one routed from a nursing home, she was brought to prison. On entering, she had to strip and leave all her clothes in a side room; she was then wrapped in a sheet and taken to the showers.

> Next we were ordered to take an enema and to climb on an examination table for examination. All openings of the body were roughly searched for narcotics by "a doctor"—a large woman who made insulting remarks about Communists who did not appreciate this country. I told her to mind her business. Once she became so animated in her opinions while she was taking a blood specimen that she allowed the blood to run down my arm. "Watch what you are doing," I said. "Never mind my politics, watch my blood."

Refusing to cooperate with the government in naming her associates in the party, she was sentenced to the federal penitentiary, where she remained from January 1955 to May

1957. A famous case involving her and the Marxist historian Herbert Aptheker brought a legal victory before the Supreme Court and enabled her to travel abroad. In the early 1960s, she visited several times in the Soviet Union. When she died in Moscow, on September 5, 1964, she received a state funeral in Red Square.

In a long, eventful, and often stormy public life, Flynn participated in most of the major struggles for justice during the first half of the century. Her autobiography, *The Rebel Girl* (1976), gives a detailed and instructive account of the education of a woman whose life was lived for the benefit of others. She gave up easier and more conventional careers in order to side with the workers, a choice that, as Dorothy Day wrote later, had religious implications:

> Gurley Flynn was of the laity, and she was also my sister in the deep sense of the word. She always did what the laity is nowadays urged to do. She felt a responsibility to do all in her power in defense of the poor, to protect them against injustice and destitution.

The title of Flynn's autobiography is taken from a song written for her by Joe Hill, the Swedish immigrant laborer and Wobblie balladeer. She had come to Hill's defense when he was arrested and brought to trial, as she had for so many young radicals; and Hill's words, later set to a ragtime tune, are a fitting tribute to "the rebel girl":

> There are women of many descriptions
> In this queer world as everyone knows.
> Some are living in beautiful mansions,
> And wearing the finest of clothes.
> There are blue-blooded queens and princesses,
> All dressed in diamond and pearl.
> But the only and thoroughbred lady
> Is the rebel girl.

By Elizabeth Gurley Flynn

The Alderson Story: My Life as a Political Prisoner. New York: International Publishers, 1963.

The Rebel Girl: An Autobiography—My First Life (1906-1926). New York: International Publishers, (1955) 1973.

About Elizabeth Gurley Flynn

Camp, Helen C. "Flynn." *Notable American Women: The Modern Period: A Biographical Dictionary.* Ed. Barbara Sicherman and Carol Hard Green. Cambridge, MA: Harvard University Press, 1980.

Day, Dorothy. "Elizabeth Gurley Flynn." *By Little and by Little: Selected Writings by Dorothy Day.* Ed. Robert Ellsberg. New York: Alfred A. Knopf, 1983.

Randolph Bourne (1886-1918)

In the 1920s and 30s, many writers and intellectuals remembered the First World War as a tragic, even pointless error; but during the four long years of the "senseless slaughter," as Ernest Hemingway called it, few of them publicly opposed the war. Bertrand Russell, who lost his Cambridge University fellowship and went to prison because of war resistance, was a dissenter; so was Randolph Bourne, who endured harassment and neglect because of his public opposition to American intervention. The theme of his essays, critical of Woodrow Wilson and the war fever, was summarized in an ironic phrase, "War is the health of the State."

In the postwar decade, Bourne was a guiding spirit for young writers and artists in Greenwich Village and influenced the "new" *Dial*, 1920-29, edited by his admirer, Schofield Thayer. Since then, such diverse social critics as Theodore Dreiser and John Dos Passos, Edward Dahlberg and Noam Chomsky have regarded Bourne as a model of honesty and personal courage and as an intellectual hero of the 20th century.

Born in Bloomfield, New Jersey, on May 30, 1886, Randolph Bourne was physically disfigured at birth and progressively deformed later by spinal tuberculosis, but this deformity seldom impeded his vigorous, multi-faceted early career. After high school, where he indicated a talent for writing and a keen interest in the social sciences, he worked in factories and offices in New Jersey and New York City for four years before entering Columbia University on scholarship in 1909. Harsh conditions among workers and the precariousness of their lives shaped the sensibility of the young writer and prompted his commitment to socialism during his undergraduate years.

In 1913, an article on youth in *Atlantic Monthly* brought Bourne to the attention of editors and readers; that summer, he completed an M.A. degree at Columbia and left on a traveling fellowship to Europe. He returned from there on the eve of the war, having witnessed the chaos that led to "the guns of August," 1914. For the next three years he worked hard, but unsuccessfully, to keep America neutral; and his essays between April 1917 and the armistice in 1918 charted the effects of the war fever on the youthful spirit of the times, and prophesied the disillusionment that was to characterize the post-war period. He died during the flu epidemic of December 1918 at 33 years of age.

"Call this thing that goes on in the modern schoolroom schooling, if you like. Only don't call it education." This was the first of several "disagreeable truths" that Bourne preached to his readers, in this case from the pages of the first issue of the *New Republic* magazine, November 7, 1914; over the next four years, until his premature death, he applied his vigorous intelligence to American politics and culture in a manner that was both original and prophetic. In the pages of the "old" *Dial* and *Seven Arts*, he stood almost alone in condemning America's entry into World War I. In essays on education and the State, on the "new" poetry, fiction, and film, he also left a unique record of one man's struggle against intellectual conformity and the war-making state.

An admirer of William James and a student of John Dewey, Bourne brought a wide range of interests and experience to his discussion of "trans-national America," a **165** country shaped by the immigrant migrations of the late 19th and early 20th centuries. His reflections on the promises and perils of the American experience focused on institutions such as the schools and the university, as well as on the arts—the poetry of Vachel Lindsay and Amy Lowell, the fiction of Willa Cather and Theodore Dreiser, the art of the cinema. He embraced early modernism as an appropriate response to the new century and as a corrective to the cold intellectualism of the 19th century social engineers.

For Bourne, the new pragmatism, in the writings of John Dewey (who supported the war), simply revived the old hazards of Puritanism, with its insensitivity to feeling and its self-righteousness. Such forces, masked as modern liberalism, squandered America's emotional capital, Bourne said, and perpetuated old errors. In sinning against the spirit of American promise, the social philosophers guided the nation "through sheer force of ideas into what the other nations entered only through predatory craft or popular hysteria or militarist madness." For Bourne, America's active participation on the side of Great Britain and France ended any chance of its providing balance in an unstable world.

Bourne opposed the war not as an isolationist or idealist, but as an enlightened realist, since America's military involvement prevented it from serving as an arbiter between the Allies and the Central Powers. In "Below the Battle," he described a young man victimized by the intellectual and social forces of a nation at war. Though not afraid to die for his country, the youth obviously had no hatred of the enemy, Bourne argued, "even when the government decided that such animus is necessary to carry out its theories of democracy and the future organization of the world." Conscripted to fight, the draftee will go, but in the work of annihilation his youthful skepticism will turn to bitterness, Bourne said. And so it did.

In the midst of the war, Bourne came to understand the excesses of the modern state and the consequences for peacetime, especially the usurpation of the individual conscience by institutions established during times of stress. Under such tyranny, he argued, the desire for personal freedom becomes the impersonal instinct of the herd for conformity, creating a "conscience" no longer capable of distinguishing between good and evil, but only between what is acceptable to the state and what is unacceptable. His theme was to recur in numerous works later in the century, in such diverse writings as George Orwell's *Nineteen Eighty-Four*, Albert Camus's *The Rebel*, and Gordon Zahn's *German Catholics and Hitler's Wars*. In the Red Scare of 1919, when American radicals and labor agitators were imprisoned and exiled, Bourne's worst fears were confirmed.

In writing about cultural issues, Bourne drew upon his knowledge in many areas, the philosophy of education, adolescent psychology, political theory, and literary criticism. His artistic sensibility, attentive to the new directions in music and poetry, as well as fiction and film, enabled him to absorb the full impact of the war, when many of his contemporaries ignored its aesthetic and moral implications.

Bourne's portraits of young conscripts in his essays, for example, strongly resemble the fictional characters in the novels of the "lost generation" shortly afterward. And there are close similarities between the conscripts described in his anti-war essays and the three young Americans in John Dos Passos's novel *Three Soldiers* (1921), Frederick Henry in Ernest Hemingway's *A Farewell to Arms* (1929), and the disillusioned and psychologically troubled narrator of Robert Graves's memoir, *Goodbye to All That* (1929). Though older by several years, Bourne spoke a language similar to that of the soldiers in Wilfred Owen's ironic poems, "Futility" and "Dulce et Decorum Est Pro Patria Mori" (It is sweet and just to die for one's country).

In his honesty, "his relying on analysis rather than on rationalizations or ideologies," as Olaf Hansen has said, Bourne focused his attention on immediate experience rather than on abstract concepts or preconceived ideas. He treated culture and society as something lived rather than as something passively accepted.

167

A posthumously published "The History of a Literary Radical" described the intellectual tradition, from Thomas Paine to William James, that sustained Bourne in his social criticism. He called it "the new classicism," combining literary art and social thought, which he thought held promise for the future:

> Finding little in the American tradition that is not tainted with sweetness and light and burdened with the terrible patronage of bourgeois society, the new classicist will yet rescue Thoreau and Whitman and Mark Twain and try to tap through time a certain eternal human tradition of abounding vitality and moral freedom and so build out the future.

Bourne, a model for later social critics, redeemed the times by appreciating what the times made available, while refusing to be their prisoner.

By Randolph Bourne

The Radical Will: Randolph Bourne Selected Writings, 1911-1918. Ed. Olaf Hansen. New York: Urizen Books, 1977.

War and Intellectuals: Collected Essays, 1915-1919. Ed. Carl Resek. New York: Harper and Row, 1964.

About Randolph Bourne

Moreau, John Adams. *Randolph Bourne: Legend and Reality.* Washington, D.C.: Public Affairs Press, 1966.

Schlissel, Lillian. *The World of Randolph Bourne.* New York: E.P. Dutton and Co., 1965.

Bertrand Russell (1872-1970)

Recognizing Bertrand Russell as a moral leader of this century is somewhat complicated by the fact that he was also one of its famous scoundrels. A characteristic remark in this vein was his comment to a woman friend in 1947: "How right you are about chastity. I gave it a good try once, but never again." An appropriate response from another woman friend was that if Russell thought that he was the nearest man could get to being God, he was close to being Satan as well.

Russell's refusal to endorse the war fever during World War I was, nonetheless, a courageous assault on the moral indifference of that period. For his pacifism, he lost a major fellowship at Cambridge University; from then until his death in 1970, at ninety-eight, he effectively exposed the immorality of pompous and pious Christians. While they went off to war, killing their brothers and sisters on the other side with easy consciences, Russell, the agnostic, withheld his approval and suffered the consequences of his dissent. With impressive logic and enviable humor, he won a permanent place in the history of movements for social justice, calling nations and their leaders to task for their inhumanity to one another and fostering a moral regeneration on issues of war and peace during the dark ages following World War II.

Although hesitant at times about supporting widespread civil disobedience, he was nonetheless an advocate of direct action, arguing in *Which Way to Peace?* (1936) that

> all great advances have involved illegality. The early Christians broke the law; Galileo broke the law; the French revolutionaries broke the law; early trade unionists broke the law. The instances are so numerous and so important that no one can maintain as an absolute principle obedience to constituted authority.

Or, as he said at the time of World War I: "I don't know how one can advocate an unpopular cause unless one is either irritating or ineffective."

Born in Revenscrot, Monmouthshire, England, on May 18, 1872, Bertrand Russell was reared by his grandmother, Lady Russell, wife of the former prime minister under Queen Victoria. His parents had both died by the time he was four. His brother Frank gave "Bertie" his first lessons in Euclid, which thrilled him and led to his early love of mathematics. After private tutoring, he entered Trinity College, Cambridge University in 1890, and was elected a fellow there five years later. The following year he married an American woman, Alys Smith, the first of four marriages, and traveled to the United States.

Elected a Fellow of the Royal Society in 1908, Russell collaborated with Alfred North Whitehead on *Principia Mathematica* (1910), and continued to lecture widely in Europe. Support for a conscientious objector and agitation against England's entrance into World War I got him into trouble. He lost his fellowship in 1916, and for writing against the war he later served six months in Brixton Prison, where he wrote *Introduction to Mathematical Philosophy*. The attitude that overtook him, as news about the slaughter on the Western Front poured in, surprised him.

> I have at times been paralyzed by skepticism, at times I have been cynical, at other times indifferent, but when the

Randolph Bourne   Emma Goldman

Eugene Victor Debs   Jane Addams

war came I felt as if I heard the voice of God. I knew that it was my business to protest, however futile protest might be. . . . As a lover of truth, the national propaganda of all the belligerent nations sickened me. As a lover of civilization, the return to barbarism appalled me. As a man of thwarted parental feeling, the massacre of the young wrung my heart.

In the early 20s, Russell traveled to Russia, China, and Japan, and ran for parliament as a member of the Labor Party. After a second marriage and parenthood, he returned to lecture several times in the United States, and in 1931, on the death of his brother, he became the Third Earl Russell, though he rarely used his title. In 1940, he gave the William James lectures at Harvard, an inquiry into meaning and truth, and then was refused permission to teach at the College of the City of New York because of his political and moral views. Re-elected to a fellowship at Trinity College, Cambridge, he continued to lecture widely both in his native country and abroad. In 1949, he was awarded the Order of Merit by the British government; and in 1950, he received the Nobel Prize for Literature, "in recognition of his many-sided and important work in which he constantly stood forth as a champion of humanity and freedom of thought."

Internationally famous at 30, Russell was destined for immortality from the beginning, and the books by and about him are legion. His friends, associates, and students included many famous people of his time: Aldous Huxley, T.S. Eliot, Ludwig Wittgenstein, D.H. Lawrence, John Maynard Keynes. Sometimes regarded as the greatest logician since Aristotle, he combined a skeptical turn of mind with wicked wit and regarded "impersonal non-human truth as a delusion." A rationalist even in his eighties, he thought neither misery nor folly had any part in the inevitable lot of man. "And I am convinced that intelligence, patience, and eloquence can, sooner or later, lead the human race out of its self-imposed torture provided it does not exterminate itself meanwhile."

172 But, the quality which gives Russell special claim on one's attention is his persistence in the pursuit of peace and justice.

"Seldom indeed," wrote Daniel O'Connor, "has a philosopher shown such a sense of responsibility."

Faithfulness in upholding values of social justice has, of course, characterized the lives of many heroes of nonviolence. One thinks of Dorothy Day, at 78, arrested in California in support of the United Farm Workers; Ammon Hennacy, at 76, picketing the capitol building in Salt Lake City against capital punishment; and Eugene Victor Debs, at 65, serving a three-year sentence in Atlanta federal prison for draft resistance. Among those who persisted, however, Bertrand Russell, Nobel laureate and lord of the realm, may hold the record. Jailed at 89 for planning a demonstration advocating unilateral disarmament, he said later, "What I want is some assurance before I die that the human race will be allowed to continue." There were, at the same time, his speeches at rallies in Trafalgar Square against apartheid and against nuclear weapons, and the initiation of the Campaign for Nuclear Disarmament, which continues to thrive, more active than ever, in England and other European countries.

By Bertrand Russell

The Autobiography of Bertrand Russell, 3 Vols. New York: Allen Unwin, 1967, 1968, 1969.

The Basic Writings of Bertrand Russell. Ed. Robert E. Egner and Lester E. Dennon. New York: Simon and Schuster, 196L

Why I Am Not a Christian and Other Essays on Religion and Related Subjects. New York: Simon and Schuster, 1957.

Portraits from Memory and Other Essays. New York: Simon and Schuster, 1956.

About Bertrand Russell

Clark, Ronald W. *The Life of Bertrand Russell.* New York: Alfred A. Knopf, 1976.

Mohandas Gandhi (1869-1948)

"This is the man," Romain Rolland said of Gandhi in 1924, "who has stirred three hundred million people to revolt, who has shaken the foundations of the British Empire, and who has introduced into human politics the strongest religious impetus of the last two hundred years." But the most unusual tribute to Gandhi is undoubtedly George Orwell's, shortly before his death in 1950. Suspicious of pacifists and vegetarians, Orwell had to overcome most of his instincts to find anything good in a person venerated by so many: "Saints," his "Reflections on Gandhi" begins, "should always be judged guilty until they are proved innocent, but the tests that have to be applied to them are not, of course, the same in all cases."

After putting Gandhi to the test, Orwell comes down clearly on the side of the Mahatma ("great soul"), with a comment on his ability to "disinfect" the political air, as India and Great Britain settled down to decent and friendly relations. "One may feel, as I do, a sort of aesthetic distaste for Gandhi," Orwell said, and regard his basic aims "as anti-human and reactionary; but regarded simply as a politician, and compared with other leading political figures of our time, how clean a smell he has managed to leave behind!"

This rather minimalist endorsement of one of the great teachers of nonviolence is instructive, since it dramatizes the conflicting attitudes aroused by even the most consistent pacifist. It suggests as well how little is known and understood still about nonviolent approaches to social change.

In a relatively brief history, nonviolence made a great leap forward, nonetheless, during and through Gandhi's experiments with truth; and his writings, as well as the scholarship about him, provide the most extensive record available of its history. Among the items central to students are the film of Richard Attenborough, *Gandhi* (1982) and the psychoanalytic study, *Gandhi's Truth*, by Erik Erikson.

Mohandas Karamchand Gandhi was born on October 2, 1869, in Porbandar, India, on the Kathiawar peninsula, where his father was prime minister of the region. Married, according to custom, at thirteen, Gandhi attended Samaldas College, after completing the local high school. In 1888, leaving his wife and child, he sailed for England, where he was admitted to the Inner Temple to learn the law. Completing his studies and called to the bar in 1891, he returned to India, still rather infatuated with English tradition and finery.

Unsuccessful in his practice at home, Gandhi sailed for South Africa as an adviser to a Muslim in 1893. There, he became active as an organizer in various associations and served in the ambulance corps during the Boer War. In 1903, after two years in India and the birth of his fourth son, he returned with his family to South Africa. Taking a vow of chastity at this time, he became more deeply involved, through his law practice in Johannesburg, in seeking a redress of grievances for Asians in South Africa. By this time he knew the essays of John Ruskin and Thoreau's "Civil Disobedience"; he also translated Tolstoy's *Letter to a Hindu* and established Tolstoy Farm, for Indian resisters. Imprisoned on several occasions, Gandhi was nonetheless successful in campaigns against discrimination, and by the time he returned to India in 1914, he was well-known in his home country. In 1909 he had written, while in jail, that one of the inner struggles of his life was "to bring Hindus and Muslims together."

In 1915, Gandhi founded his own ashram, a retreat for communal living, near Ahmedabad, in northern India, and began a campaign on behalf of millworkers. That continued, with mass civil disobedience, through the 1920s. His goal by this time was Indian independence from Great Britain, as well as peaceful co-existence between Hindus and Muslims. In prison, he wrote Satyagraha in South Africa, published essays in numerous periodicals, and read daily in the *Bhagvad Gita*.

In the early 1930s, following the proclamation of the Indian Declaration of Independence, Gandhi was imprisoned on several occasions, and in 1932, he announced a fast unto death in protest against the treatment of untouchables. His efforts for independence, which included a successful trip to England, continued through the early years of the Second World War. The struggle led to his and his wife's imprisonment, where they remained until her death in February 1944, and his release the following May. In 1947, he initiated another fast to bring an end to religious strife in India. A year later, on January 30, 1948, he was assassinated by a radical Hindu, as he moved through a crowd at Birla House, in New Delhi.

"We must widen the prison gates, and we must enter them as a bridegroom enters the bride's chamber. Freedom is to be wooed only inside prison walls and sometimes on gallows, never in council chambers, courts, or in the schoolroom," Gandhi wrote. The extent of his influence as a thinker is suggested by the frequency with which such statements serve as a source of inspiration and guidance for resisters throughout the world. This particular one provided the title for Philip Berrigan's fourth book, *Widen the Prison Gates*, written during his own imprisonment between 1970 and 1972. For almost every civil disobedient for justice in the later 20th century, Gandhi, that "seditious Middle Temple lawyer and half-naked fakir," as Winston Churchill called him, has been a presence, a person to be contended with, either challenged or imitated.

Martin Luther King, Jr., in a famous photograph from the Civil Rights movement, is seated beneath a picture of Gandhi; and Daniel Berrigan, S. J., recorded his own reflections during his time in federal prison, in *Lights on in the House of the Dead*.

Lucy Stone   Mohandas Gandhi

Leo Tolstoy   Henry David Thoreau

Numerous Americans have gone to India to learn how to appropriate Gandhi's spirit and tactics to later struggles for justice. The Reverend Carl Kline, who initiated peace witness of citizens from the United States on the borders of Nicaragua and Honduras, conducts such a pilgrimage as an apostle of satyagraha (truth-seeking).

Long after his death, Gandhi's influence still manages, as Orwell said, to "disinfect" the political air. Martin Luther King, Jr., Gandhi's principal American disciple, regarded his approach to social change as the only practical one for a nuclear age, for as King wrote, "The choice is clearly between nonviolence and nonexistence."

By Mohandas Gandhi

An Autobiography: The Story of My Experiments with Truth. Boston: Beacon Press, 1962.

Gandhi's Experiments with Truth: Essential Writings By and About Mahatma Gandhi, Ed. Richard L. Johnson. New York: Rowman and Littlefield Publishers, Inc., 2006.

About Mohandas Gandhi

Erikson, Erik H. *Gandhi's Truth: On the Origins of Militant Nonviolence*. New York: W.W. Norton and Co., 1969.

Fischer, Louis. *Gandhi: His Life and Message for the World*. New York: New American Library, 1954.

Payne, Robert. *The Life and Death of Mahatma Gandhi*. New York: E.P. Dutton and Company, 1969.

Emma Goldman (1869-1940)

After organizing against the draft during the First World War, Emma Goldman, Alexander Berkman, and 247 others were deported from the United States in 1919. That repressive measure was a project of an ambitious young lawyer named J. Edgar Hoover, who regarded Goldman and Berkman, her lover, as "two of the most dangerous anarchists in this country." Their principal "crime" was in regarding themselves —as Thomas Paine and William Lloyd Garrison did before them—as "citizens of the world." In her commitment to the common good, Goldman followed the dictates not of the State, but of her conscience. She took seriously the advice of Walt Whitman in *Leaves of Grass*: "Resist much, obey little. Once unquestioning obedience, once fully enslaved."

In message and tone, Goldman's introduction to her autobiography (1913), "In Appreciation," is representative. Acknowledging her gratitude to those who came into her life for several hours or several years, she wrote, "Their love, as well as their hate, has gone into making my life worthwhile." In demonstrations, speeches, and vigorous, readable essays, she warned against the dangers of highly centralized power, **179** including the violence and oppression resulting from a managerial elite. As she said in the popular pamphlet *What I Believe* (1908), anarchists were the only ones calling a halt "to the growing tendency of militarism, which is fast making of this erstwhile free country an imperialistic and despotic power." With Eugene Victor Debs, the Industrial Workers of the World, and similar militants in the worker's struggle, Goldman helped to make the period before the First World War perhaps the most vibrant era in American political history. During her adventurous life and since her death, her example has helped to make other lives "worthwhile," as various tributes suggest.

In his *One Man Revolution in America* (1970), Ammon Hennacy named her one of the eighteen greatest Americans, and Dorothy Day, who "longed to walk in the shoes of Mother Jones and Emma Goldman," made Goldman's anarchist principles central to the Catholic Worker movement. Theodore Dreiser regarded Goldman's writings as "the richest of any woman's of the century," and John Dewey and Bertrand Russell thought her an important and attractive personality, as did many European anarchists. The playwright S.N. Behrman wrote affectionately about her in his memoir *The Worcester Account*, and Stanley Kunitz, in the poem "Journal to My Daughter," brags of belonging to "a flinty maverick line," that welcomed Goldman, Ingersoll, and other radicals to the family table, also in Worcester. Howard Zinn, the historian, wrote a successful play about her in the 1970s, and feminist critics regard her as a forerunner of the women's movement. In 1970, young members of the Emma Goldman Brigade marched down Fifth Avenue in New York City chanting: "Emma said it in 1910. Now we're going to say it again," according to Alix Kates Shulman.

Born June 27, 1869, in Kovno, Lithuania, Emma Goldman was the third child of Taube Bienowitch, and the first of three children by her second husband, Abraham Goldman. Emma Goldman attended a Jewish elementary school where she excelled academically, before moving to St. Petersburg, where the family's poverty forced her to take a full-time job in a factory at thirteen. Two years later, partly because of her father's threat to marry her off, she fled with her sister to America.

At her first job, in Rochester, New York, Goldman sewed overcoats for ten hours a day at $2.50 a week. In the U.S., as in Russia (where she had seen peasants beaten), she was appalled by the horrible conditions of workers. In 1886, she was deeply affected by the unjust conviction and eventual hanging of four Chicago anarchists in the famous Haymarket Square trial, writing later:

> I had a distinct sensation that something new and wonderful had been born in my soul. A great ideal, a burning faith, a determination to dedicate myself to the memory of my martyred comrades, to make their cause my own.

After a brief marriage to another Russian immigrant and still only twenty years old, she moved to New York City and became the protege of Johann Most, the anarchist editor of *Freiheit*. Working later as a seamstress, Goldman became a leading organizer for at cloak-maker's strike in 1889. Like many anarchists of the time, she thought that the masses could be aroused to revolt against their masters by some dramatic, polarizing event. In 1892, when Pinkerton guards shot into striking steelworkers at the Carnegie plant, in Homestead, Pennsylvania, Alexander Berkman resolved to assassinate the chairman of the company, Henry Clay Frick. When the attempt failed and Berkman went to prison for fourteen years, Goldman defended him. She became a major spokesperson for anarchism and spent a year in prison for "inciting a riot" that never occurred; in actuality, in an argument resembling that of medieval theologians, she had merely justified the "stealing" of bread by starving people.

Following a period of repression at the turn of the century (after an anarchist killed President McKinley), Goldman returned to public life again in 1906, the year she launched *Mother Earth*, a monthly supporting feminism, free speech, and similar issues. She published essays on Ibsen, Strindberg, and **181**

Shaw, whose plays she regarded as powerful dramatizations of the plight of women, as well as anarchist classics by Kropotkin and Bakunin, writings by Oscar Wilde, and her own essays on anarchism and literature.

While giving herself tirelessly to various campaigns for workers' rights and women's rights, she was also a success on the lecture circuit, speaking 120 times in thirty-seven states during 1910, for example. "Combative by nature," Alix Kates Shulman wrote, Goldman "talked up free love to puritans, atheism to churchmen, revolution to reformers; she denounced the ballot to suffragists, patriotism to soldiers and patriots." In 1915, she spent fifteen days in jail for giving a public lecture on methods of birth control in support of Margaret Sanger.

When America entered the war against Germany in 1917, Goldman and Berkman—now out of prison—formed the No-Conscription League, which led to their arrest for conspiring to obstruct the draft. The league maintained that "the militarization of America is an evil that far outweighs, in its anti-social and anti-libertarian effects, any good that may come from America's participation in the war." In a characteristically witty and courageous speech to the judges, Goldman described the methods of the arresting officer and "his host of heroic warriors" as being sensational enough to satisfy the famous circus men, Barnum & Bailey....

> A dozen or more heroes dashing up two flights of stairs prepared to stake their lives for their country, only to discover the two dangerous disturbers and trouble-makers, Alexander Berkman and Emma Goldman, in their separate offices, quietly at work at their desks, wielding not a sword, nor a gun or a bomb, but merely their pens! Verily, it required courage to catch such big fish.

(The arresting officers' behavior resembled that of the F.B.I. harassing and arresting draft resisters during the Vietnam war; on Block Island in 1970, for example, Daniel Berrigan was arrested by F.B.I. agents disguised as birdwatchers.)

182   During the Red Scare of 1919, J. Edgar Hoover, later head of the F.B.I., directed hearings for Goldman's deportation, after

revoking her citizenship. Under the 1918 Alien Exclusion Act, he shipped Goldman, Berkman, and 247 other radicals on the Buford, an old army transport, to the "new" Soviet Union.

Initially enthusiastic about the Bolshevik Revolution of 1917, Goldman became one of its fiercest critics when she realized that in the U.S.S.R., as in many other countries, anarchists were treated as enemies of the State. Moving to France in the early 1930s, then to England, and during the Spanish Civil War to Spain, she directed the anarchist press there. Rising to speak in a crowded hall, amid anarchist cheers, fascist boos, and communist cat-calls, she countered them by announcing "that she had had fifty years of dealing with mobs and no one could shout her down. And by God she was right," says Ethel Mannin, an English novelist, who adds that the crowd sat "enchanted under the attack, and when she had finished applauded wildly."

Traveling to Canada to raise money for Spanish anarchists in 1939, Goldman suffered a stroke and died some months later in Toronto, May 14, 1940. Karl Shapiro, in "Death of Emma Goldman," has pictured her in her final moments, surrounded by officials who had hounded her during her adventuresome life:

> Triumphant at the final breath
> Their senile God, their cops,
> All the authorities and friends pro tem
> Passing her pillow, keeping her concerned.

In actuality, she never bowed before authorities and adversaries who denounced, exiled, and imprisoned her; as a great advocate for social justice, loyal to her values and her radical friends, she seldom faltered.

Only in death was Goldman finally allowed to re-enter the United States to be buried in Chicago's Waldheim Cemetery, near the graves of her beloved Haymarket martyrs. Once asked for details about her life, Goldman suggested that the person consult "any police department in America or Europe."

By Emma Goldman

Red Emma Speaks: Selected Writings and Speeches of Emma Goldman.
Ed. Alix Kates Shulman, ed. New York: Vintage Books, 1982.
Living My Life. 2 Vols. New York: Dover Publications, (1931) 1970.

About Emma Goldman

Drinnon, Richard. *Rebel in Paradise. A Biography of Emma Goldman.*
Chicago: University of Chicago Press, 1961.
Falk, Candance S. *Love, Anarchy, and Emma Goldman: A Biography,*
Rev. ed. New Brunswick, N.J.: Rutgers University Press, 1990.

Jane Addams (1860-1935)

In 1917, Theodore Roosevelt called her the "most dangerous woman in America." Five years before, she had seconded his nomination for president as a candidate of the Progressive Party, and welcomed her support in his (unsuccessful) campaign. Five years before that, Roosevelt had helped to initiate one of the first inter-governmental peace conferences, a project that she carried further in co-founding the Women's International League for Peace and Freedom.

Roosevelt, like other conventional Americans, admired Jane Addams for co-founding Chicago's Hull House in 1889; but he was shocked when she committed herself to something as "radical" as resisting the war effort in 1915. Such were the shifting, changing responses to one of the great leaders in the American tradition of nonviolence: a person who learned as she went along, taking whatever action seemed appropriate, no matter what the public response.

Although she enjoyed the praise that accompanied her work among poor immigrants, Addams repeatedly risked censure—and the loss of public favor—in addressing the causes of poverty and working for peace during a "popular" war. Her defense of political radicals, especially when the Justice

Department imprisoned or exiled them to Europe during the Red Scare of 1919, is particularly noteworthy. "Providing a voice of reason in the midst of hysteria," as Michael A. Lutzger has said, she defended the loyalty of aliens in Chicago and the liberties they had lost:

> The cure for the spirit of unrest in this country is concili- ation and education—not hysteria. Free speech is the greatest safety valve of our United States. Let us give these people a chance to explain their beliefs and desires. Let us end this suppression and spirit of intolerance which is making America another autocracy.

Born September 6, 1860, in Cedarville, Illinois, Jane Addams was the eighth of nine children of Sarah Weber and John Huy Addams. Her mother died when Addams was three years old. Her father, a successful miller and eight-term state senator, encouraged Addams to attend Rockford Female Seminary (now Rockford College) near Chicago, where she excelled as a student and won the admiration of her contempo- raries. Among various Victorian writers whom she admired, John Ruskin, art historian and social critic, occupied a special place. Following several bouts of ill health in the 1880s, she left Woman's Medical College in Philadelphia after one semester and traveled extensively in Europe on two occasions.

On the second tour, accompanied by Ellen Cates Starr—later a co-founder of Hull House—Addams was deeply impressed by Toynbee Hall, a settlement house in London's East End where university students influenced by Ruskin taught workers and learned from them as well. Although she had long thought about fulfilling an early Christian commitment to the welfare of the poor, she associated her vocation as a social reformer with extensive reading on that subject after her return from England.

Subsequently, Addams and Starr convinced a number of educated women to support their determination to live among the poor in Chicago, where three-fourths of the residents were foreign born. After moving into an old mansion in the heavily populated and predominantly Italian West Side in September

186

1889, Addams, Starr, and their co-workers provided or arranged for childcare, educational programs, and medical assistance for neighborhood immigrants. During the early weeks, they found themselves caring for "a forlorn little baby who, because he was born with a cleft palate, was most unwelcome even to his mother" and later died of neglect, and for "a little Italian bride of fifteen" who sought shelter with them in order to escape her husband's nightly beatings.

> Two of us officiated quite alone at the birth of an illegitimate child because the doctor was late in arriving, and none of the honest Irish matrons would "touch the likes of her"; we ministered at the deathbed of a young man who, during a long illness of tuberculosis, had received so many bottles of whisky through the mistaken kindness of his friends that the cumulative effect produced wild periods of exultation, in one of which he died.

The community of educated women and college students gathered around Hull House provided programs in the arts as well as the elemental necessities for those in need. Faculty from the new University of Chicago (Robert Morss Lovett); editors and artists who initiated a Chicago Renaissance (Margaret Anderson); socialists and anarchists (Sidney and Beatrice Webb and Peter Kropotkin); workers and scientists "from the river wards of the city" and "from the far comers of five continents"—all contributed to the noble experiment and the spirit of community emerging from it. Within four years of the founding of Hull House, Addams and other notable women were assisting and entertaining 2000 people a week in a variety of functions and activities, including theater performances and musical concerts.

In the wider community, Hull House exerted considerable influence on movements for child labor laws, unions, and workers' benefits. In 1909 Addams was elected the first woman president of what would become the National Conference of Social Work; in 1910, she was the first woman to receive an honorary degree from Yale University and published her most widely read book, *Twenty Years at Hull House*, still widely read.

187

Traveling extensively in this country and abroad over the next half-century, Addams nonetheless made Hull House her home for the remainder of her life.

Spurred by the enthusiasm of the progressive era, the women's movement, and powerful ideas associated with Early Modernism, Addams had become increasingly interested in international issues. Visiting Leo Tolstoy, Russian novelist and Christian anarchist, in 1896, made a deep impression on her. Although his eating peasant porridge and black bread—while his guests dined in style—made her uncomfortable, she took to heart his teachings about justice and community as the bases of world peace. During the Spanish American War two years later, Addams—like William and Henry James, Mark Twain, and Andrew Carnegie—joined the Anti-Imperialist League and began to note the links between violence among Chicago's immigrant poor and violence implicit in America at war.

Haltingly, and in a manner that disconcerted admirers of Hull House, Addams became increasingly involved in efforts to build nongovernmental organizations committed to world peace. Inevitably, as a result of these efforts, she became embroiled in controversy. To an impressive social vision linking religious, moral, and aesthetic concerns, Addams added another concern: the disastrous effects of war on social reform.

With the outbreak of the war in August 1914, she worked hard at home and abroad to keep the U.S. neutral so that it might serve as a mediator between the two warring groups. In 1915, as head of the Woman's Peace Party, she traveled the Western front and met with various leaders in an attempt to stop what Ernest Hemingway called "the senseless slaughter."

Over the next two years, Addams watched Woodrow Wilson's gradual drift toward war and the country's inevitable and increasing belligerence regarding it. Wilson and his advisers thought active involvement would strengthen his hand in settling the peace—a naïve belief, as Addams maintained and as it turned out to be. In the midst of increasing **188** criticism from the Daughters of the American Revolution, American Legion, and similar self-appointed patriots, Addams persisted—as did Eugene Victor Debs, Emma Goldman, Bertrand Russell, Randolph Bourne—in pointing to the disastrous effects of an uncritical endorsement of war policies.

Before the armistice in 1918, Addams was already working to distribute food and to provide relief in war-torn countries. The International Congress of Women, which had met in the Hague during and in Zurich just after the war, included many women who survived the war only to face additional hardships. Warning that the Versailles peace settlement sowed the seeds of another war, the women formed a permanent organization, the Women's International League for Peace and Freedom (WILPF), with Addams as president. In spite of criticism, she continued to work with other groups committed to nonviolence and the protection of human rights, including the National Association for the Advancement of Colored People (NAACP), American Friends Service Committee (AFSC, and American Civil Liberties (ACLU). It was to WILPF, however, that she gave the money accompanying her Nobel Prize for Peace in 1931.

By that time, some of the criticism that had dogged Addams since she announced herself a pacifist in 1915 was muted or forgotten. Never entirely comfortable with her commitment to pacifism, she worked persistently, patiently, modestly, nonetheless, to understand its implications for social change. In 1922, describing the isolation she felt among friends supporting the war, she indicated why she remained faithful to that lonely, often misunderstood, nonviolent ethic: "in order to make the position of the pacifist clear it was perhaps necessary that at least a small number of us should be forced into an unequivocal position." In doing so, Addams offered a number of models for peacemaking and nonviolence, in practicing what Taylor Branch has called "an orphan among democratic ideas."

By Jane Addams

Peace and Bread in Time of War. New York: Garland Publishing Co, **189**
1922 (1972).

Twenty Years at Hull House. New York: Signet Classics, 1910 (1960).

About Jane Addams

Bussey, Gertrude, and Margaret Times. *Women's International League for Peace and Freedom 1915-1965: A Record of Fifty Years' Work.* London: George Allen & Unwin, 1965.

Davis, Allen. *American Heroine. The Life and Legend of Jane Addams.* New York: Oxford University Press, 1973.

Peace Heroes in Twentieth-Century America. Ed. Charles DeBenedetti, Bloomington: Indiana University Press, 1986.

Eugene Victor Debs (1855-1926)

In his social biography of Eugene Victor Debs, Nicholas Salvatore warns that, too often, Debs is regarded as a "larger-than-life hero," as someone born eternally at odds with the culture around him. Such a view does violence to Debs's full story, especially to the indigenous nature of his radicalism, nurtured as it was by the land, period, and tradition he shared with many Americans—Thomas Paine, William Lloyd Garrison, and Dorothy Day among them.

Debs was a product of the American experience and his hope in the reconstruction of the social order resembled that of settlers from the 17th century to the present. At twenty-eight, for example, still under the influence of William Riley McKeen, whom Debs called "the model railroad president," he gave this ringing endorsement of America as "preeminently the land of great possibilities, of great opportunities, and of no less great probabilities. . . .We all have a fair chance and an open field. Long may it so remain. The time, the occasion is auspicious. Nothing like it was ever known before."

Such a statement is as representative of the man as his later and more famous statement at his sentencing for draft resis- **191** tance in 1918: "While there is a lower class, I am in it; while there is a criminal element, I am of it; and while there is a soul in prison, I am not free." Five times the Socialist party's nominee for president of the United States, Debs received a significant percent of the vote on two occasions. Warren G. Harding, elected president in 1920, released Debs from Atlanta prison; earlier Woodrow Wilson had granted amnesty to other political prisoners after the war ended in 1918, but not to the popular Debs.

Ammon Hennacy, in Atlanta prison for draft resistance at about the same time, regarded Debs and Malcolm X as the two greatest Americans in history. Hennacy admired Debs for his courage, but also for his faithfulness to the poor and the down-and-out. Debs' dedication to the railroad workers and the Wobblies (I.W.W.) did not end once he became a popular leader. He was not running for office or seeking a power base from which to launch a political career; he was a leader who cast his lot with workers and who remained loyal to them to the end.

Born on November 5, 1855, in Terre Haute, Indiana, where his parents had settled several years after immigrating from Alsace-Lorraine, Debs left school at fifteen to work on the railroad. Within five years he was secretary of the local Brotherhood of Locomotive Firemen. In 1885, the year of his marriage to Katherine Metzel, he was elected to the Indiana legislature as a Democrat, where he voted for measures that would now be regarded as anti-union.

In 1893, Debs helped to form the American Railway Union and subsequently became its president. The next year, when employees of the Pullman Company went out on strike, he took charge of the campaign, after some initial reservations, and later served a six month prison sentence in the McHenry County (Ill.) jail for refusing to abide by a court injunction against the strikers.

In jail, a reading of Marx and Engels further radicalized Debs, and within four years, he was nominated for president by the Socialists. Shortly afterward, he became an editor of the party's weekly, *Appeal to Reason*; published in Girard, Kansas, it eventually achieved a circulation of over 800,000. In the summer of 1905, in Chicago, Debs co-founded the Industrial Workers of the World, with Mother Jones, Lucy Parsons, and Big Bill Haywood; and although he later disagreed with the Wobblies, he always supported their right to organize. During the presidential campaign of 1908, Debs drew large crowds speaking from a train known as the "Red Special," and in the election of 1912, he polled almost a million votes, a figure exceeded in the election of 1920, when he campaigned from federal prison. A large following in Oklahoma, led by Mary Kate O'Hare, lobbied for his eventual release in 1921.

Debs' arrest in Canton, Ohio, in 1918, at a Socialist state convention, followed several warnings about his speaking against wartime conscription; but he believed strongly in the party's policy and its slogan, "Don't be a soldier, be a man." Sentenced to ten years for violation of the Espionage Act, he was one of many victims of the so-called Red Scare, during that repressive era in American history. (The actions of the Attorney General and an ambitious young lawyer named J. Edgar Hoover led to the deportation of Emma Goldman and two hundred and forty "radicals" in 1919 and the harassment and denial of basic civil liberties to many others.)

Although he remained active to the end, the time in prison weakened Debs' health. Back in Terre Haute he wrote articles on prison conditions, published later as *Walls and Bars*, and continued leadership of the Socialist party. When he died in October 1926, 10,000 people attended the funeral services, and his home in Terre Haute is now a memorial to a man admired and loved by many. In 1971, when she received the annual Debs award, Dorothy Day spoke at his gravesite, acknowledging his influence on her own life, as a friend of the poor and as a writer and worker for social justice.

Among Debs' contributions to social history, as Nick Salvatore points out, were his understanding of the complex character of the democratic tradition and his ability to re-define it for the twentieth century. Integrating social and economic themes in a way that his audience understood, Debs recognized **193** the central place of the class struggle and of social protest in

American history, without ignoring cultural and religious traditions. "Christ," Debs argued, "organized a working class movement. . . for no other purpose than to destroy class rule and set up the common people as the sole and rightful inheritors of the earth." In this and similar statements, Debs showed his mastery of political and religious exhortations characteristic of American oratory since the time of the Puritans. In his personal example, as well as in his national leadership, he is, as Salvatore says, "a constant reminder of the profound potential that yet lives in our society and in ourselves."

By Eugene Victor Debs

Debs. Ed. Ronald Radosh. Englewood Cliffs, New Jersey: Prentice Hall, 1971.

Eugene V. Debs Speaks. Ed. Gene Y. Tussey. New York: Pathfinder Press, 1970.

Walls and Bars. Chicago: C.H. Kerr, (1927), 1973.

About Eugene Victor Debs

Ginger, Ray. *The Bending Cross: A Biography of Eugene Victor Debs*. New Brunswick, New Jersey: Rutgers University Press, 1949 (1962).

Salvatore, Nick. *Eugene V. Debs: Citizen and Socialist*. Urbana, IL: University of Illinois Press, 1982.

Leo Tolstoy (1828-1910)

In the history of nonviolence, Tolstoy and Gandhi occupy special places; among Americans, only Dorothy Day and Martin Luther King, Jr. enjoy such distinction. It was Tolstoy who confirmed the reputations of several American theoreticians: William Lloyd Garrison, Henry David Thoreau, and Adin Ballou, whose writings Tolstoy cited after his own conversion to "non-resistance," as he called it, in 1880. From then until his death in 1910, he wrote numerous letters, essays, and pamphlets that constitute a major library on the subject.

Tolstoy argued with such authority on the scriptural and biblical evidence for Christian nonviolence as to almost single-handedly transform a religious tradition or at least to redirect a significant minority of believers. Since then, many Christians have re-interpreted the social and political implications of their faith. Nonviolence, one might say, is the 19th century counterpart to liberation theology, which has had a similar effect in emphasizing the social implications of Christianity in recent times.

For Americans, Tolstoy's pamphlets have particular significance, since some are based upon his reading of 19th century abolitionists and anarchists whom he admired. **195**

If I had to address the American people, I would like to
thank them for their writers who flourished about the
fifties . . . . And I should like to ask the American people
why they do not pay more attention to these voices
(hardly to be replaced by those of financial and industrial
millionaires, or successful generals and admirals), and
continue the good work in which they made such hopeful
progress.

In a famous polemic, *The Kingdom of God Is Within You*
(1894), Tolstoy spoke of the American Quakers who responded
to his writings on nonviolence and he quoted extensively from
Garrison's "Declaration of Sentiments Adopted by the Peace
Convention" (1838) in Boston. Tolstoy also corresponded with
Adin Ballou, the founder of the Hopedale Community, and
perhaps the first major theorist of nonviolence, or what he
called "non-resistance," in 1846.

At a time when politicians justify an increase in nuclear
weapons as a means of encouraging peace negotiations (the
infamous "build-down theory" of the Reagan administration,
for example), Tolstoy's conclusion to *The Kingdom of God Is
Within You* seems especially relevant:

It has often been said that the invention of the terrible
military instruments of murder will put an end to war,
and that war will exhaust itself. This is not true. . . . Let
them be exterminated by thousands and millions, let them
be torn to pieces, men will still continue like stupid cattle
to go to the slaughter, some because they are driven
thither under the lash, others that they may win the
decorations and ribbons which fill their hearts with pride.

In his pamphlets, as in the earlier novels, Tolstoy
combined a practical and naturalistic eye for detail with a
theoretical and moral vision. And at the end of his polemics, he
returned to the central question posed by most Russian writers
and intellectuals of the 19th century: "What is to be done?" In
"Letter to the Liberals" (1896), for example, he answered that
elemental question in this way:

Merely the simple, quiet, truthful carrying on of what you consider good and needful, quite independently of government and of whether it likes it or not. In other words: standing up for your rights, not as a member of the Literature Committee, not as a deputy, not as a landowner, not as a merchant, not even as a member of Parliament; but standing up for your rights as a rational and free man, and defending them, not as the rights of local boards or committees are defended, with concessions and compromises, but without any concessions and compromises, in the only way in which moral and human dignity can be defended.

Born in Russia, on August 28, 1828 (old-style calendar), at Yasnaya Polyana, the family estate where he is buried, Leo Nikolayevich Tolstoy was the fourth son of Count Nikolai Ilyich Tolstoy. Reared by an aunt after the death of his mother and father, he studied briefly at Kazan University, and as a young man spent much of his time gambling and drinking. Later, after studying law, he established a progressive school for children of the serfs on his estate. His first stories were published during his years in the army, at the time of the Crimean war. Leaving the army in 1856, he traveled about Western Europe, principally France and Germany. In 1863, the year after his marriage, he began work on *War and Peace* (1869). Various essays and fiction followed, including a second major novel, *Anna Karenina* (1878). Although his later fiction is sometimes regarded as inferior to these novels, its popularity steadily increases, particularly *The Death of Ivan Ilyitch* (1886), *The Kreutzer Sonata* (1890), and *Resurrection* (1899).

Internationally famous at fifty, Tolstoy suddenly suffered from bouts of deep despair. In 1879 he wrote,

My question was the simplest of questions lying in the soul of every man from the foolish child to the wisest elder: It was a question without an answer to which one cannot live, as I had found by experience. It was "What will come of what I am doing today or shall do tomorrow? What will come of my whole life?"

197

Re-reading the Old and New Testaments at this time, Tolstoy experienced a conversion to radical Christianity. Subsequently, he wrote extensive commentaries on the Bible, blaming the decline of Christianity, after Constantine, on the church's failure to live up to the religious pacifism of Jesus. Christianity had failed, Tolstoy argued, because it refused to disassociate itself from political power, the sanctification of which he regarded as blasphemous, as the negation of Christianity. "In truth, the words a 'Christian state' resemble the words 'hot ice.' The thing is either not a State using violence, or it is not Christian," he argued.

In 1888, following the birth of her thirteenth and last child, Tolstoy's wife and his chief disciple, Chertkov, quarreled. From then until the end of his life, the conflicts in the household worsened, as Tolstoy devoted himself to fiction, to Christian anarchism, and to the defense of his followers, the Dukhobors, who were exiled to Canada in 1899. In 1910, in the midst of another crisis at home, Tolstoy left Yasnaya Polyana and, on November 7 of that year, died of pneumonia at Astapovo, at age eighty-two. At his funeral two servants carried a banner at the head of the procession that read, "Dear Leo Nikolayevich, the memory of your greatness will not die among us, the orphaned peasants of Yasnaya Polyana."

Tolstoy's writings document the close relationship between peace and justice issues; and perhaps because he was writing to a most unsympathetic audience, in an era when the very idea of nonviolence was foreign to many Christians, his arguments retain their intensity and vigor a century later. For that reason, almost everyone committed to nonviolence, from Gandhi to the Catholic Worker movement, from Martin Luther King, Jr., to the youngest draft resister, regards Tolstoy's pamphlets as basic texts.

Of the two great Russian novelists, Tolstoy and Dostoevsky, one usually thinks of Dostoevsky as the more anguished, the person severely tested by the dichotomies of life, and by the evils to which human beings subject one **198** another. But as a prince, as an aristocrat who had much to lose by his conversion, Tolstoy spent much of his later life on a pilgrimage. He died miles from his home, still searching, one might say, for the proper way to live his life as a Christian pacifist.

By Leo Tolstoy

The Portable Tolstoy. Ed. John Bayley. New York: Penguin Books, 1978.

Tolstoy's Writings on Civil Disobedience and Non-Violence. New York: Bergman Publishers, 1967.

About Leo Tolstoy

Simmons, Ernest J. *Introduction to Tolstoy's Writings.* Chicago: University of Chicago Press, 1967.

Steiner, George. *Tolstoy or Dostoevsky: An Essay in the Old Criticism.* New York: Alfred A. Knopf, 1959.

Troyat, Henri. *Tolstoy.* Tr. Nancy Amplioux. Garden City, New York: Doubleday and Co., 1967.

Abigail Kelley (1811-87)
Stephen Symonds Foster (1809-81)

The disappearance of significant figures from standard American histories robs successive generations of models for moral and political responsibility. As a consequence, married couples who decided to center their lives on justice issues seldom hear about past examples of how to live their lives. In some instances, men and women sacrifice their spouses in order to follow vocations for social justice. In others, one of them lives in the background, maintaining the family and caring for the children, while the other pursues a public life. In a few instances, however, husbands and wives successfully maintain two vocations, the one to the social order and the one to one another. This was particularly true of Abigail Kelley and Stephen Symonds Foster, both of whom appear in the *Dictionary of American Biography*, though Abby is generally regarded as the more famous of the two.

Both people, however, deserve a special place in the history of nonviolence, she as an abolitionist, feminist, and tax resister, he as a faithful apostle of nonviolence, abolitionist, and war resister. Their correspondence both before their marriage and during the years each stayed at home, while the other took to the circuit on behalf of abolitionism, is a remarkable record of a union that was oppressive to neither, that was liberating for both. That respect and love are reflected in a tribute Stephen wrote for Abby late in their lives: "O, how I wish she could be young again, to thrill the very air with her fiery denunciations . . . . Her work, I fear, is nearly done on earth, but she has large investments in Heaven. In moral power I have never known her equal, and never shall."

Each of them came to marriage in 1845 with a dedication to social justice and something of a career based upon these concerns. Abby had advocated immediate abolition of slavery since the early 1830s, when she first heard William Lloyd Garrison speak, and Stephen had taken various risks in resisting slavery and militarism since his undergraduate days at Dartmouth College.

Born in Pelham, Massachusetts, on January 15, 1811, Abigail Kelley was the daughter of Irish Quakers. She attended schools in Worcester, Massachusetts, where her parents, prosperous farmers, moved soon after Abby was born, as well as the Friends School in Providence, Rhode Island. At the time she heard Garrison, she was teaching in Lynn, Massachusetts, and later headed a five-woman delegation to the National Female Anti-Slavery Society convention in New York. In 1839, she left teaching altogether in order to devote full-time to abolitionism, confessing to Theodore Weld at the time that she had "nothing to start upon, nothing to commend me to the notice or favor of any, no name, no reputation, no script, neither money in my purse."

Abby Kelley proved, nonetheless, to be an effective champion of the cause, traveling throughout New England, New York, and into the Midwest, speaking to large and appreciative audiences, and co-editing *Anti-Slavery Bugle*. Frequently she was ridiculed for speaking to "promiscuous" audiences (that is, audiences of men and women), and for traveling about with men, both black and white. But she remained faithful to her motto: "Go where you are least wanted, for there you are most needed." **201**

The very qualities that scandalized conventional souls were the ones that attracted Stephen Foster. As a vigorous and independent agitator for justice, he had long faced the kind of opposition that he occasionally provoked. Born in southern New Hampshire, on November 17, 1809, the ninth of twelve children, Stephen Symonds Foster graduated from Dartmouth College in 1838 and went to study for a time at Union Theological Seminary in New York. He had been jailed in Hanover, New Hampshire, for refusing to perform military duty at college, and left Union when the administration refused permission for a room to hold an anti-war meeting. Later, as an itinerant preacher, he traveled New England, asking to speak to congregations, particularly if they had not endorsed abolitionism, and in 1843 he published a popular pamphlet entitled *The Brotherhood of Thieves; or, A True Picture of the American Church and Clergy*. It argued that any church that refused to condemn slavery was "more corrupt and profligate than any house of ill fame in the city of New York . . . ."

The 1850s were particularly hectic years for the Fosters, with Stephen and then Abby on speaking tours, while the other cared for their daughter, "Alla," born in 1847. That decade saw the first National Woman's Rights Conventions at Seneca Falls, New York, in 1848, and in Worcester, in 1850 and 1851, in which Abigail had an active part. During these years, particularly because of the Fugitive Slave Law of 1850, the Foster home in Worcester was a busy station on the underground railway. In 1854 an incident involving a federal marshal, who came to arrest a former slave, and the Worcester Vigilance Committee, which resisted him, tested Stephen's dedication to nonviolence. With two others, Foster escorted the arresting officer through a hostile crowd of abolitionists and onto a train back to Boston, to protect him from harm. In a letter to Abigail, Stephen described the conflict within himself; as an abolitionist, he opposed everything the officer stood for, but as a pacifist, he could not allow anyone to assault him.

I have often been myself the object of popular rage, as you well know, but never did I feel half the anxiety for my

Adin Ballou   Thomas Paine

Stephen Symonds Foster   Abigail Kelley

own life which I felt for his, or make half the effort to save it. There, I felt that the honor of our cause was at stake, and for the moment, my heart yearned almost with agony for a bloodless victory.

The Fosters were also tax resisters, maintaining that they owed no allegiance to a government which allowed Abigail no vote and little voice in its proceedings. Only in old age, when Stephen was ill and Abigail was exhausted from a lifetime of agitation, did they finally pay the taxes to regain a title to their land. Stephen died in 1881 and Abigail in 1887, in Worcester; their home, near Tatnuck Square, is preserved and named on the National Register.

Wendell Phillips said of Stephen, who was noted for his resonant voice and his colorful denunciations of slaveholders, "It needed something to shake New England and stun it into listening. He was the man, and offered himself for the martyrdom." A writer for the *Woman's Journal* wrote, at the time of Abigail's death:

> The women of this land owe this woman more than to any other human being, a debt of gratitude for the doors she opened for them to enter, for the paths she made smooth for them with her own bleeding feet, for the courage and conscientiousness and faithfulness with which, amid persecution and reviling, she made the way clear for them to walk safely.

And best of all, the Fosters' marriage was a happy one, both for the couple and for abolitionism, as Abigail wrote to a female friend: "I wish to congratulate the cause on the fact that since our marriage, meetings have been much more successful than heretofore. We realize that even in the anti-slavery cause a whole man and a whole woman arc far better than a half-man and a half-woman."

By Stephen Symonds Foster

The Brotherhood of Thieves, or a True Picture of the American Church and Clergy. New York: Arno Press, 1863, 1866 (1969).

About Abigail Kelley and Stephen Symonds Foster

Bacon, Margaret Hope. *I Speak for My Slave Sister: The Life of Abby Kelley Foster.* New York: Thomas Y. Crowell, 1974.

Burkett, Nancy. *Abby Kelley Foster and Stephen S. Foster.* Worcester, Mass.: Worcester Bicentennial Commission, 1976.

Melder, Keith E. "Abigail Kelley Foster." In *Notable American Women, 1607-1950: A Biographical Dictionary*, Vol. I. Ed. Edward T. James and Janet W. James. Cambridge, Mass.: Harvard University Press, 1971.

Sterling, Dorothy. *Ahead of Her Time: Abby Kelley and the Politics of Slavery.* New York: W.W. Norton, 1994.

Henry David Thoreau (1817-62)

"In the mountains where Henry David Thoreau preached civil disobedience," the news story began, "some stiffnecked tax resisters are locked in a battle of will with U.S. authorities over an isolated house."(In protesting against U.S. military interventions around the world a century later, Randy Kehler and Betsy Corner waged "a battle" by refusing to pay federal income taxes on their home. Going Thoreau one better, they gave the tax money to victims of war, homelessness, and injustice.)

Subsequently, supporters in the Western Massachusetts village of Colrain risked arrest by occupying the 91-year-old house after Kehler was carried away to jail; in doing so, they joined an estimated 10,000 people throughout the U.S. who resist federal taxes that pay for war and nuclear armaments. Some knowingly, others unknowingly, perhaps, followed the "good ole American" precedent set by Thoreau and others 150 years before.

In 1846, Thoreau was provoked to active resistance by U.S. intervention in Mexico, in this country's first major imperialist war; Kehler and Comer were provoked by U.S. interventions in El Salvador, Panama—those successive, relentless imperial sorties during the 1980s, as they were provoked earlier by

Korea, Vietnam, Grenada, Nicaragua. Kehler, forty-seven years old at the time of his arrest in December 1991, had spent 22 months in federal prison for draft resistance during the decade-long war in Southeast Asia.

Although Henry David Thoreau regarded himself as a mystic and natural philosopher, he has probably pushed more people into action than have most so-called revolutionaries. Born in 1817 in Concord, Massachusetts, Thoreau ventured from his native city only occasionally, but—like his contemporary Emily Dickinson of Amherst—learned more from his relatively circumscribed life than most people learn by traveling the world. His approach to mining nature's secrets during two year's residence at Walden Pond, then along the Concord and Merrimack Rivers, to Maine and Cape Cod remains as valid today as it was in the mid-19th century. "I went to the woods because I wished to live deliberately," he wrote in *Walden*, "to front only the essential facts of life...

> I wanted to live deep and to suck out all the marrow of life ... to drive life into a comer, and reduce it to its lowest terms, and, if it proved to be mean, why then to get the whole and genuine meanness of it, and publish its meanness to the world; or if it were sublime, to know it by experience, and be able to give a true account of it in my next excursion.

Prior to his two years at Walden Pond in the 1840s, Thoreau had grown up in Concord, graduated from nearby Harvard College, then returned to live with his family and to teach school in Concord, where he also became a close associate of Emerson and other members of the Transcendental Club and wrote for *The Dial* magazine. After the sojourn at Walden Pond, he stayed in Concord, writing and making occasional trips to Maine, Cape Cod, and New York (where he met Walt Whitman), and—in the early 1860s—to the Great Lakes and along the Mississippi River. He died in 1862, at 45, of tuberculosis.

One can hardly overemphasize the timeliness of Thoreau's **207** writings at present, as well as in the 19th and 20th centuries. For citizens, he provides a vigorous, authoritative, and inspiring rationale for resisting a repressive, war-making State. His work often led persons very different from Thoreau in temperament and background "to construct peace." Over the two centuries, that influence has been acknowledged by nonviolent activists and theorists from Tolstoy and Gandhi to Martin Luther King, Jr., and Philip Berrigan, by Danes resisting Nazism in the 1940s, and Chinese students waging a pro-democracy movement in 1989. Reflecting on his night in jail, initially in a lecture, then in the published essay, "Civil Disobedience," Thoreau advocated an adamant stand against paying taxes that "enable the State to commit violence and shed innocent blood." He was angered, particularly Thoreau by his fellow abolitionists, perhaps including Emerson, for their failure to take a more militant stand against slavery. Emerson's uneasiness with Thoreau is evident in several journal entries at the time, as well as in their (probably apocryphal) exchange at the Concord jail: Emerson: "Henry, what are you doing in there?" Thoreau: "Waldo, what are *you* doing out *there*?"

Thoreau spoke not as a lawyer or politician, but as a moralist, because, as he said in Walden, "Our whole life is startlingly moral. There is never an instant's truce between virtue and vice. Goodness is the only instrument that never fails." He understood that those most responsible for an evil— at that time, slavery—succeed not because of their behavior, but because others who recognize the evil do nothing to stop it. "Practically speaking, the opponents of a reform in Massachusetts are not a hundred thousand politicians at the South," he said, "but a hundred thousand merchants and farmers here, who are more interested in commerce and agriculture than they are in humanity."

In "Civil Disobedience," Thoreau also challenged passive citizens who think they can have a better society merely by wishing for it. "Even voting for the right is doing nothing for it," he argued. "It is only expressing to men feebly your desire that it should prevail." Writing in his journal soon after his night in jail Thoreau said of tepid citizens, "Better are the physically dead for they more lively rot."

Rereading "Civil Disobedience," one imagines what he might say about the politics of greed and the accompanying collapse of this country's infrastructure since the Persian Gulf and Iraq wars. The fact that contemporary writers of Thoreau's stature seldom attend to today's civil disobedients as closely as he did to those of his own time speaks also of America's decline.

One can hardly take up "Civil Disobedience" without the blood stirring, without being drawn into the central issues of Thoreau's era and our own—issues that touch on the nature of government, community, individual rights, but also of language, discourse, writing, argument, rhetoric. It is such an extraordinarily rich document—vigorous, concrete, passionate, witty, philosophical, even as it provokes more questions about governance, perhaps, than it answers.

Historically, Thoreau's statement belongs to a tradition that dates from at least the 17th century and touches on arguments and cases that involved the Quakers particularly, over three centuries, in England and America. He also profited from and built upon many statements similar to his own in the years associated with the abolitionist struggle and protests against the Mexican War, by Emerson, Bronson Alcott, and the transcendentalists, and by William Lloyd Garrison and Adin Ballou. It is no accident that, in resisting imperial wars and policies since the Second World War, activists inevitably re-work some of the ground plowed by Thoreau 150 years before.

For centuries, men and women committed to nonviolence have tried to figure out ways not only to resist a system that upheld slavery and oppression, but also to prevent this country from imitating European imperialists in conducting their affairs. Although not the first such effort (David R. Weber, in *Civil Disobedience in America: A Documentary History*, includes several essays written prior to Thoreau's), "Civil Disobedience" brought together the arguments proposed by others in an eloquent and economical way; it remains, along with the Declaration of Independence and Martin Luther King, Jr.'s "Letter **209** from Birmingham Jail," the most influential document in the tradition. Even if Thoreau was not a pacifist, his stance before the State was more revolutionary than those of most recent nonviolent activists, and his argument and statement are central to anyone committed to bringing about social change.

Just how far Thoreau would go to resist the government is dramatized by his "A Plea for Captain John Brown," written a decade after "Civil Disobedience." Reflecting the intellectual and moral vigor of the 1850s, when Emerson, Hawthorne, Melville, and Whitman published other American master-pieces, the essay took a position shared by William Lloyd Garrison, Frederick Douglass, and others who came to regard the Civil War as a holy war.

In his visits to Worcester, a hot-bed of abolitionism twenty miles southwest of Concord, for example, Thoreau spoke to a sympathetic audience. Thoreau's admirers there included Thomas Wentworth Higginson, Elihu Burritt, Abigail Kelley and Stephen Symonds Foster, and other militants. Some Worcesterites, as with Bostonians and Concordians, probably found Thoreau's "A Plea for Captain John Brown," about the militant abolitionist's raid at Harper's Ferry, too radical for their taste. But characteristically, Thoreau felt compelled "to correct the tone and statements" of editors and politicians regarding Brown's character and actions. In his address, Thoreau told his audience at Mechanics Hall, Worcester, "It costs us nothing to be just."

Hardly a disciple of nonviolence, Thoreau, nonetheless, belongs to an American tradition of justice-seekers that includes John Woolman, Jane Addams, Dorothy Day, Ammon Hennacy, and David Dellinger. And since about 1960, draft resisters, the Catonsville Nine, members of Clamshell Alliance and Plowshares—have regarded Thoreau as their inspiration and guide. By their commitment to civil disobedience, in resisting injustice and war, they keep Thoreau's memory alive.

Modern scholars, including Walter Harding and Richard Lebeaux, have done their part as well, in enabling us to see the life and thought of the great moralist in context. It remains for the rest of us to see that Thoreau's words and example inform our efforts to alter the priorities of our society and government to reflect his moral and ethical concerns. We do so by resisting unjust laws and practices, as he did, and by "building a new society in the shell of the old," as the Wobblies and Peter Maurin, co-founder of the Catholic Worker movement, recommended. Individual resisters who live Thoreau's principles make a difference, if only "as a majority of one," as he said.

By Henry David Thoreau

Walden and Other Writings. Ed. William Howarth. New York: Modern Library, 1981.

Henry D. Thoreau Reform Papers. Ed. Wendell Click. Princeton, N.J.: Princeton University Press, 1973.

About Henry David Thoreau

Harding, Walter Roy. *A Thoreau Handbook.* New York: New York University Press, 1959.

Lebeaux, Richard. *Thoreau's Seasons.* Amherst: University of Massachusetts Press, 1984.

Civil Disobedience in America: A Documentary History. Ed. David R. Weber. Ithaca, N.Y.: Cornell University Press, 1978.

Civil Disobedience in Focus. Ed. Hugo Adam Bedau. New York: Routledge, 1991.

Elihu Burritt (1810-79)

How many lives were saved by John Woolman (1720-72), the abolitionist? How many by Elihu Burritt, "the learned blacksmith" and other peace activists throughout history? Yet students familiar with little-known Civil War soldiers may never have heard of Woolman and Burritt, while military commanders who sent hundreds to their deaths, in campaigns that neither settled disputes nor furthered just causes, have cities, mountains, and thoroughfares named for them. No wonder that young people sometimes complain, "We learn all about making war, and nothing about making peace."

Famous—or infamous—for its military might and nuclear weapons, the U.S. is also home to important apostles of nonviolence, as well as the first International Peace Society, founded in 1854. Elihu Burritt, one of history's most remarkable advocates of nonviolent social change, was a co-founder of that society. He worked for global peace by encouraging negotiations among countries in conflict and establishing a Congress of Nations to prevent civil and international wars. Although internationally famous in his own lifetime, he remains relatively unknown, even in the area of New England where he lived and worked for seventy years.

Born December 8, 1810, in New Britain, Connecticut, he was one of ten children of Elizabeth Hinsdale and the senior Elihu Burritt, a veteran of the Revolutionary War known for his honesty and generosity. "A poor boy," his biographer, Merle Curti, says of the younger Burritt, he shared a life of hardship with his parents, who cultivated "a few rocky, barren acres of soil" in Southern Connecticut. After the death of his father, Burritt apprenticed himself to a village blacksmith and, in the midst of his labors, read 18th and 19th century English poetry.

Delighting in the study of languages, according to his own account Burritt "made himself more or less acquainted with all the languages of Europe and several of Asia, including Hebrew, Syriac, Chaldaic, Samaritan, and Ethiopic" by the time he was thirty. Penniless, he had moved to Worcester, Massachusetts, several years before, where he borrowed grammars and lexicons from the American Antiquarian Society, established by the editor and bookseller Isaiah Thomas in 1812. Burritt's journal entry for October 7, 1841, suggests his daily schedule: "Read Ethiopic 1 hour; wrote 1 hour upon a subject which I intend to make a lecture, viz., 'Is Roman patriotism or Christian philanthropy most congenial to the Republican principle?' Got trusted for 30 pounds of cast iron to make my garden hoes of. Went to the library and read 2 ½ hours. Forged from 1 to 5 P.M. Antislavery Convention in the evening; listened to the most thrilling and powerful speeches."

When Burritt's achievement in languages became known to Edward Everett, Governor of Massachusetts, and Henry Wadsworth Longfellow, poet and professor of modern languages at Harvard University, Burritt was offered opportunities for formal study, but declined. His vocation, as he described it to Longfellow, was "to stand in the ranks of the workingmen of New England, and beckon them onward and upward ... to the full stature of intellectual men."

Through his lectures and writings, Burritt encouraged other young workingmen to study and to develop their talent for scholarship, as he had done. And during his middle and later years, from 1840 until his death in 1879, he devoted **213** himself, as writer, editor, and activist, to campaigns for abolishing slavery and improving workers' conditions, and gathered tens of thousands of signatures for a document in which Europeans and Americans promised never to take up arms against their brothers and sisters again.

From 1844 to 1851, Burritt published *The Christian Citizen*, a newspaper devoted to temperance, abolitionism, and nonviolence. During that period, he addressed International Peace Congresses on three occasions, at Brussels (1848), Paris (1849), and Frankfurt (1850). His speeches called for an international code of justice that might "give the world an ocean penny postage," helping to make the world "home" for everyone and "all nations neighbors." Although his sentiments sound naive at times, and were somewhat circumscribed by his optimistic view of Western thought, they contributed to his later, more sophisticated explorations of nonviolent theory and practice.

From 1865-69, he published the periodical *The Bond of Universal Brotherhood* in the U.S. and in England, where he served as a consular agent at Birmingham during the same period. Burritt's efforts in that post suggest his persistent dedication to the welfare of the poor. He helped to protect prospective immigrants to the U.S., for example, from unscrupulous promoters who took advantage of their clients by misrepresenting working conditions in America.

As editor of the *Advocate of Peace* and *Universal Brotherhood* for the American Peace Society, Burritt popularized the ideas of William Ladd (1778-1841), founder of the American Peace Society, which helped to shape the League of Nations and the World Court. More significantly, Burritt emphasized the importance of "people's diplomacy" and is credited with helping to avoid a war with Great Britain over the Oregon Country. Burritt's effort anticipates recent experiments in "citizen diplomacy," in addressing issues related to world hunger, nuclear war, and destruction of the environment. Groups such as Witness for Peace, Bread for the World, Physicians for Social Responsibility, Soviet and Nicaraguan 214 Sister-City Projects, and similar nongovernmental agencies indicate the wisdom of Burritt's approach.

Almost half a century before Mohandas Gandhi and the Industrial Workers of the World (Wobblies) recommended large-scale disobedience against injustice, Elihu Burritt advocated a working-man's strike against war. In a peace pledge of 1867, signed by tens of thousands of Americans and Western Europeans, he wrote, "We hope the day will come when the working-men of Christendom will form one vast Trades Union, and make a universal and simultaneous strike against the whole war system."

As with U.S. civil rights workers in the 1950s and 1960s; the June 4, 1989, pro-democracy supporters in China; or those who resisted the 1991 coup in the Soviet Union, Burritt understood the power of nonviolence. "Any community or country might employ/_it_/successfully in repelling and disarming despotism, whatever amount of bayonet power it might have at its command," he wrote in "Passive Resistance" (1854). His numerous periodicals and thirty books, according to Merle Curti, his principal biographer, describe his "manifold efforts to counteract the martial spirit." As with Randolph Bourne, who argued against the U.S. entering World War I so that it might act as an arbitrating power between the warring parties, Burritt wanted the U.S. to act as mediator in the Crimean war. Similarly, Burritt's condemnation of British and French wars in Asia anticipate Gandhi's later speeches on behalf of Indian independence.

In one of his last letters, about "the machinery of war having a central show" in the Philadelphia Centennial Exposition, Burritt indicated a keen, skeptical sense of his country's future. That letter is, in fact, somewhat prophetic of what the U.S. became a century later, as the major supplier of armaments to the world:

> For there were never so many furnaces, forges and arsenals at work, turning out the latest improvements in the machinery of war, as at the present moment, and no mind and hand more busy and ingenious in the invention and manufacture of such weapons than the American.

In later years, as his energy waned, Burritt returned to language study, received an honorary degree from Yale University, translated Longfellow's poetry into Sanscrit, and continued writing. *A Voice from the Back Pew* (1870) traced the history of his religious opinions. He died in New Britain, Connecticut, where he was born; there, on the campus of Central Connecticut State University, a library is named for him.

In efforts to resolve conflict, to bring about social change without killing, and to translate peace principles into action, Burritt occupies a special place in U.S. history. For this reason, among others, the historian Staughton Lynd regards Burritt's life and writings as the most significant contribution to the American tradition of nonviolence between the Revolution and the Civil War.

By Elihu Burritt

The Learned Blacksmith: The Letters and Journals of Elihu Burritt. and *A Congress of Nations.* Ed. Merle Eugene Curti. New York: Garland Publishing, 1971.

Thoughts and Things at Home and Abroad. Boston: Phillips, Sampson, and Co., 1854.

A Memorial Volume With Selections From the Writings and Lectures. Ed. Charles Northend, 1979.

About Elihu Burriti

Brock, Peter. *Pacifism in the United States: From the Colonial Period to the First World War.* Princeton, N.J.: Princeton University Press, 1968.

Nonviolence in America: A Documentary History. Rev. ed. Staughton and Alice Lynd, Maryknoll, New York: Orbis Books, 1995.

Tolis, Peter. *Elihu Burritt: Crusader for Brotherhood.* Archon Books, 1968.

Adin Ballou (1803-90)

Although Henry David Thoreau's "Civil Disobedience" (1849) and Martin Luther King, Jr.'s "Letter from Birmingham Jail" (1963) are the most famous documents in the American tradition of nonviolence, without Adin Ballou's "Christian Non-Resistance in All Its Important Bearings" (1846), would we have the other two? Although less well known than the other two theorists of nonviolence, in spirit, Adin Ballou is very much alive. Agape Community in Ware, Massachusetts, resembles, in fact, Ballou's Hopedale Community, a 19th-century utopian experiment in nearby Milford. For both, the nonviolent gospel combining a refusal to kill and a commitment to social justice is central.

Reading Ballou's prose, one is struck by the apparent justice of his son-in-law's description of him as "a great power for good in the world, a noteworthy man of his age." For the tone and mood of Ballou's writings have a kind of sweet reasonableness about them, particularly when one remembers the difficulties he faced in espousing "Christian non-resistance" (nonviolence), a doctrine, as he put it, so "little understood, and almost everywhere spoken against." **217**

Prior to Leo Tolstoy, Adin Ballou contributed more to our understanding of nonviolence, perhaps, than anyone in recent history, and Gandhi probably knew of Ballou's work, through his reading of Tolstoy. The Russian count furthered the insights formulated in Ballou's carefully reasoned, generous spirited, and synthesizing treatment of the subject. in *The Kingdom of God is Within You* (1893). Recognizing the controversial nature of his "unpopular doctrine," Ballou confidently and openly explored the full implications of his defense in "Christian Non-Resistance," believing it "as ancient as Christianity, and as true as the New Testament." For these reasons, characteristically, he stressed that "friends and opposers be candid, just and generous" of his exposition, approving or condemning it "solely on its own intrinsic merits or demerits."

Born April 23, 1803, in Cumberland, Rhode Island, Adin Ballou was descended from the founders of that New England colony. At eighteen, he responded to what he regarded as a supernatural call to the ministry and subsequently headed Universalist societies in New York City and Milford, Massachusetts (where his statue stands today on the town common), and traveled throughout the Northeast as a popular preacher.

Ballou's writings in *Independent Messenger* (1831-1839) influenced Unitarian/Universalist thought considerably, and pacifist and abolitionist journals, such as *The Nonresistant and Practical Christian* (1845-49), which he edited, contributed to lively anarchist debates and the growth of Utopian communities in the decade prior to the Civil War. Although Ballou regarded himself as "no antagonist to human government," his perspective challenged the basic ideologies of what we know now as state socialism or state capitalism. His position resembles Thoreau's, in "Civil Disobedience," written during the same period; for Ballou, government is "a mere cypher," with "no rightful claim to the allegiance of man."

In his remarks to a September 25, 1839, meeting of the Non-resistance Society, in Boston, Ballou addressed the question whether we must "disobey parents, patriarchs, priests, kings, nobles, presidents, governors, generals, legislatures, constitutions, armies, mobs, *all* rather than disobey

God?" His answer, resembling that of anti-war and anti-nuclear activists in recent decades, was, "We *must*, and then patiently endure the penal consequences."

In 1841, Ballou became co-founder and president of the Hopedale Community, on 250 acres of land near Milford, Massachusetts. A utopian and Christian society based upon radical principles, it was an effort "to establish a state of society governed by divine moral principles, with as little as possible of mere human restraint." There, according to its constitution, "no individual shall suffer the evils of oppression, poverty, ignorance or vice through the influence or neglect of others."

In "What a Christian Non-Resistant Cannot Consistently Do," an opening section of *Christian Non-Resistance* (1846), Ballou listed seven commandments that conscientious followers of Jesus should obey:

> He/she cannot kill, maim, or otherwise absolutely injure any human being, in personal self-defense, or for the sake of his family, or any thing he holds dear .... He/she cannot be a member of any voluntary association, however orderly, respectable or allowable by law and general consent, which declaratively holds as fundamental truth, or claims as an essential right, or distinctly inculcates as sound doctrine, or approves as commendable in practice, war, capital punishment, or any other absolute personal injury.

Ballou stated, further, that the Christian Non-Resistant must not directly or indirectly "abet or encourage any act in others, nor demand, petition for, request, advise or approve the doing of any act, by an individual, association or government" that "would inflict, *threaten* to inflict, or necessarily cause to be inflicted any *absolute personal injury*." For the informing "sub-principle of Christian non-resistance," as Ballou argued first and Tolstoy later, in *The Kingdom of God Is Within You*, is "Evil can be overcome only with good." Anticipating Martin Luther King, Jr.'s counsel to civil rights activists and civil disobedients a century later, Ballou said "*Resist not personal injury with personal injury.*" And in a verse concluding his

219

introduction, Ballou describes Isaiah's vision, much in the manner of Edward Hick's well-known painting, "The Peaceable Kingdom":

The earth, so long a slaughter-field,
Shall yet an Eden bloom;
The tiger to the lamb shall yield,
And War descend the tomb:
For all shall feel the Saviour's love,
Reflected from the cross—
That love, that non-resistant love,
Which triumphed on the cross.

A vigorous debater, with a remarkable sense of the theoretical and practical implications of nonviolence, Ballou is at his best in addressing arguments justifying self-preservation. If self-preservation is the best method of protecting and preserving human life, Ballou asks, why have "fourteen thousand millions of human beings been slain by human means, in war and otherwise?" From such evidence, might one not conclude that such methods of self-preservation are "the off-spring of a purblind instinct—the cherished salvo of ignorance—the fatal charm of deluded credulity—*the supposed preserver*, but the real *destroyer* of the human family?"

If only a few thousands, or even a few millions, had perished by the two-edged sword;...for if the sword of self-defense had frightened the sword of aggression into its scabbard, there to consume in its rust; then might we admit that the common method of self-preservation was the true one. On the other hand, if everyone since the conflict of Cain and Abel had responded to robbery, murder, and killing with non-resistance, "would as many lives have been sacrificed, or as much real misery have been experienced by the human race," as has resulted from the usual method of responding to injury with injury?

As with so many of Ballou's arguments and questions, this **220** reflection seems more timely, more pertinent in any discussion of a "just" war today than it was a century ago. And the recent republication of his books may yet win for him the wide and thoughtful audience among activists and scholars that he deserves.

The most remarkable example of Adin Ballou's faithfulness to nonviolence was perhaps his steadfastness, as other abolitionists and non-resisters came to justify the violent means of John Brown in his raid on Harper's Ferry in 1859 and of the national government's "war to end slavery" shortly afterward. One by one, Ballou's old friends and fellow non-resistants drifted away, forgot their earlier commitment to nonviolence — William Lloyd Garrison, Thomas Wentworth Higginson, even that most persistent nonviolent activist, Stephen Symonds Foster.

In his autobiography, Ballou set their earlier statements beside their later justifications of war. Almost alone among his old radical friends, he continued to insist on just means for just ends, carefully thinking through, for example, what his grandson's response to the wartime draft should be, as a non-resistant. In the last years of his remarkably active life as writer, lecturer, and clergyman, he devoted himself to writing his family and community history, but he never repudiated or turned away from the values and principles associated with resistance to violence and discrimination that had informed his life and writings since he first formulated them fifty years before.

By Adin Ballou

Autobiography of Adin Ballou, 1803-1890, Containing an Elaborate Record and Narrative of His Life From Infancy to Old Age, with Appendixes. Ed. William S. Heywood. Philadelphia: Porcupine Press, (1896) 1975.

Christian Non-Resistance, Ed. Lynn Gordon Hughes, with an Introduction. Providence: Blackstone Editions, (1846) 2003.

History of the Hopedale Community, From Its Inception to Its Virtual Submergence in the Hopedale Parish. Ed. William S. Heywood. Lowell, Mass.: Thompson & Hill, 1897.

Practical Christianity: An Epitome of Practical Christian Socialism, Ed. Lynn Gordon Hughes. Providence: Blackstone Editions, (1854) 2002.

About Adin Ballou

Patterns of Anarchy: A Collection of Writings on the Anarchist Tradition. Ed. Leonard I. Krimerman and Lewis Perry. New York: Anchor Book, 1966.

Thomas Paine (1737-1809)

Among those who spent their lives advocating peace with justice, few names are nobler than that of Thomas Paine. English by birth, but American by choice and temperament, he called himself "a citizen of the world." His motto: "My country is the world; to do good is my religion." To a remarkable degree Paine's life and writing are one, after he discovered his particular genius as a pamphleteer on issues of liberty and social justice.

As a literary radical, Paine brought his background as a working class citizen to everything he wrote, from his first pamphlet advocating higher wages for overworked and underpaid civil employees, to *Common Sense*, *Rights of Man*, and *Agrarian Justice*. Throughout, he exhibited a talent for making complex ideas, economic and political truths, understandable to a large audience, and his writing were among the first best-sellers in the U.S. His list of humanitarian causes reads like a list of democratic movements of the past three centuries: abolitionism, land reform, women's rights, better conditions for workers, resistance to imperialism, civil rights. Although occasionally impudent and impetuous in his personal behavior, **223** he remained faithful to common folk to the end of his life, championing their cause and working in their interest. Many poor people benefited from his generosity and not a few tyrants suffered because of his forthrightness in his dedication to the truth.

Thomas Paine (spelled originally without the "e") was born in Thetford, seventy miles northeast of London, on January 29, 1737. His mother, an Anglican, was the daughter of an attorney; his father, a Quaker, was a small farmer and staymaker. In Paine's life and writings, his Quaker association remained significant, as the French radical, Marat, spitefully pointed out years later. When Paine voted against the execution of Louis XVI, in the French assembly, Marat claimed Paine did so because Quakers opposed capital punishment. For practical reasons, many Frenchmen regretted afterward their failure to follow Paine's advice.

After several years of schooling, the young Paine worked as an apprentice in his father's shop, went to sea, married, and became an excise officer in the town of Lewes. Widowed by one woman, he married again, only to be legally separated shortly afterward.

In 1773, Paine's friend, Benjamin Franklin, provided references for the younger man's move to the American colonies. A little over a year later, in Philadelphia, he published *Common Sense*, which helped to unite the colonies against a common foe, and to fan the fires of revolution first in America and then abroad.

Two years later, his *Crisis* papers championed the American cause against Great Britain and won support among the merchant class for the Revolution. George Washington and others praised Paine's papers as central to the American victory, and although congress eventually voted Paine a stipend for his writing, a statement in *American Crisis II* described his usual generosity:

> My writing I have always given away, reserving only the expense of printing and paper, and sometimes not even that. I never courted fame or interest, and my manner of

life, to those who know it, will justify what I say. My study is to be useful.

Paine subsequently alienated many powerful politicians by exposing lies and deceit in the new government; and in later years, only Thomas Jefferson remained loyal to him. As with his later attacks on superstition and traditional religion, his exposes of political skullduggery prejudiced early commentators, especially the Federalists, against him.

Away from America between 1787 and 1802, Paine played a significant role in the French Revolution, and nearly lost his life for opposing the extreme policies of Robespierre. In prison outside Paris, he continued writing essays and poems, read and revised *The Age of Reason*. Earlier, *Rights of Man* (1791), an attack on Edmund Burke and a defense of the French Declaration of the Rights of Man and the Citizen, led to charges of sedition in his native England, from which he was banished, narrowly escaping imprisonment in 1792.

The Age of Reason: Being an Investigation of True and of Fabulous Theology (1794-96) attempted to purge institutional religion of its abuses, "lest in the general wreck of superstition, of false systems of government, and false theology, we lose sight of morality, of humanity, and of theology that is true." The book caused a furor in Europe, as well as in the United States, after Paine's return in 1802. He died seven years later, on June 8, 1809, in Greenwich Village, New York City.

A scurrilous biography shortly after Paine's death provoked controversy over his life and writings once again, and later critics, such as Theodore Roosevelt, mistakenly regarded Paine as an atheist. Yet against all detractors, Paine's own defense, in response to a royal proclamation suppressing *Rights of Man*, accurately described his central concerns:

> If, to expose the fraud and imposition of monarchy, and every species of hereditary government—to less the oppression of taxes—to propose plans for the education of helpless infancy, and the comfortable support of the aged and distressed—to endeavor to conciliate nations to each other—to extirpate the horrid practice of war—to promote

225

universal peace, and civilization, and the commerce—and to break the chains of political superstition, and raise degraded man to his proper rank—if these things be libellous, let me live the life of a Libeller, and let the name of LIBELLER be engraved on my tomb.

For subsequent libertarians, William Lloyd Garrison and Walt Whitman, Eugene Victor Debs and Randolph Bourne, Paine was an inspiration and a guide, and his writing espouses values and programs still associated with nonviolent social change.

Like many American radicals, Paine hated privilege and pretension, and reacted strongly against anything that smacked of condescension toward the down-and-out, among whom he spent his earliest years. He was, to the end of his days, the supreme democrat, and his eloquent indictment of poverty, from *Agrarian Justice*, speaks to the economic injustice of the present world, as it did two centuries ago:

> The rugged face of society, checkered with the extremes of affluence and want, proves that some extraordinary violence has been committed upon it, and calls on justice for redress. The great mass of the poor in all countries arc become an hereditary race, and it is next to impossible for them to get out of that state themselves. . . . It is not charity but a right, not bounty but justice, that I am pleading for. The present state of civilization is as odious as it is unjust. . . . The contrast of affluence and wretchedness continually meeting and offending the eye is like dead and living bodies chained together.

By Thomas Paine

The Complete Writings of Thomas Paine, 2 Vols. Ed. Philip Foner. New York: The Citadel Press, 1945.

Thomas Paine: Representative Selections, with Introduction, Bibliography, and Notes. Ed. Harry Hayden Clark. New York: Hill and Wang, 1961.

About Thomas Paine

Aldridge, Alfred Owen. *Man of Reason: The Life of Thomas Paine*. Philadelphia: J.B. Lippincott Co., 1959.

Fennessy, R.R. *Burke, Paine, and the Rights of Man: A Difference of Political Opinions*. The Hague, 1963.

Foner, Eric. *Tom Paine and Revolutionary America*. New York: Oxford University Press, 1976.

Hawke, David Freeman. *Paine*. New York: Harper and Row, 1974.

True, Michael. "Thomas Paine." In *American Writers*, supplement 1, part 2. Ed. Leonard Unger. New York: Charles Scribner's Sons, 1979, 501-25.

Quakers, Mennonites, &
Church of the Brethren

In the past, they evoked fury, even hatred, from conventional Christians who were perplexed by the refusal of Quakers, Mennonites, and Brethren to take up arms against their "enemies." Today, members of the three historic peace churches are regarded as experienced, even inspiring peacemakers.

Through personal suffering in the face of community indifference or hostility, they set the pattern for conscientious objection to war and to other practices that undermined their religious commitment to peace. Thousands of Quakers, Mennonites, and Brethren suffered death and imprisonment, in this country and abroad, for conscientiously refusing to kill their brothers and sisters, whatever the justification given by the State.

How many Americans know the heavy price paid by members of the historic peace churches in helping to guarantee our free exercise of religion? In the Massachusetts Bay Colony, for example, Quakers were automatically imprisoned on their arrival in the colonies; and four of them, including Mary

Dyer—whose statue overlooks the Boston Common—were hanged for returning to Boston to worship as they pleased. In the same period, a young servant girl and a middle-aged mother of five children, after being transferred from shipboard to prison, were stripped naked, searched for witchcraft, and held for five weeks in darkness.

Quakers persisted, nonetheless, showing immense courage in upholding their rights as citizens. While William Leddra was being considered for the death penalty, Wenlock Christison, who had already been banished on pain of death, calmly walked into the courtroom. And while he was being tried, Edward Wharton, ordered earlier to leave the colony or lose his life, wrote of his decision to remain to the authorities.

In 17th-century Virginia as well, Quakers were regarded as "unreasonable and turbulent ... teaching and publishing lies, miracles, false visions, prophecies and doctrines." In the 18th century, Thomas Paine ridiculed Quakers who refused to take up arms in the revolutionary struggle against the English; and in the 19th century, Nathaniel Hawthorne, that most principled of storytellers, characterized Quakers as troublemakers threatening to rend the delicate social fabric of the new nation.

Among the Mennonites, resolutions adopted by a 1961 General Conference in Pennsylvania echo their theology and the statements by other peace churches since 1725:

1. Our love and ministry must go out to all, whether friend or foe.
2. While rejecting any ideology which ... seeks to destroy the Christian faith, we cannot take any attitude or commit any act contrary to Christian love....
3. If our country becomes involved in war, we shall...avoid joining in any wartime hysteria of hatred, revenge, and retaliation.

Together with this refusal to kill went a commitment to "justice for all." The Mennonites, for example, were among the first to resist slavery in the U.S.; one account describes an 18th-century Mennonite who slept in the forest rather than **229** accept hospitality from a slaveholder.

Although relatively small in comparison with other religious groups—the Quakers, for example, the largest of the three memberships, number only 120,000 in the U.S.—the peace churches have exercised an influence on American political traditions out of all proportion to their numbers. Famous libertarians who grew up in Quaker households include Thomas Paine, John Woolman, John Greenleaf Whittier, Lucretia Mott, Walt Whitman, and Susan B. Anthony.

Whatever liberties Americans enjoy—relating to freedom of assembly and the press and conscientious objection—have their beginnings in the witness and persistence of the historic peace communities. The principle of conscientious objection alone, first recognized in Rhode Island and, in 1940, under Selective Service laws and regulations initiated at that time, owes much to the peace churches and to related organizations initiated at the time of the First World War.

The Society of Friends (Quakers) dates from 1652, when George Fox (1624-91) gathered a group of Seekers and other Children of Light around him in England. Although not all those Quakers were pacifists, within eight years, at the time of the Restoration of Charles II, they declared to the King:

> We utterly deny all outward wars and strife and fighting with outward weapons, for any end or under any pretence whatsoever, and we do certainly know, and so testify to the world that the spirit of Christ, which leads us into all Truth, will never move us to fight and war against any man with outward weapons, neither for the kingdom of Christ, nor for the kingdoms of this world.

Later in the 17th century, William Penn (1644-1718), another Englishman jailed for his pacifist beliefs, founded a large and influential Quaker community in the American colonies. In 1681, before coming to the colonies, he summarized the general philosophy of the peace churches in a letter to Native Americans, saying that God "made the world and all things therein ... not to devour and destroy one another, but [to] **230** live soberly and kindly together in the world." He generally agreed with his contemporary, Edward Burroughs, who thought that Quakers "must obey God only and deny active obedience for conscience's sake, and patiently suffer what is inflicted upon us for our disobedience of men."

William Penn's hope for the New World, his vision, was based upon a famous passage from the Book of Isaiah, whereby the lion and the lamb would lie together, and all of nature would live in harmony. Edward Hicks, an 18th century Quaker painter—and later artists such as Fritz Eisenberg (1901-90)— popularized that image on canvas, in woodcuts and lithographs, in many versions of "The Peaceable Kingdom." Members of the Society of Friends who have been central figures of major social movements in the U.S. since Penn include John Woolman Susan B. Anthony, Abigail Kelley Foster, Lucretia Mott, and Rufus Jones.

Understanding how that vision might be lived out has been a three-century effort of trial and error, action and meditation, commitment and hesitation by these small communities of believers. How and when, in conscience, must one "stick up for God," as Ammon Hennacy used to say, and when may one "render unto Caesar"? While Christian churches justified "killing for Christ," with arguments formulated by apologists such as Augustine and other "just war" theorists, Quakers, Mennonites, and Brethren, in association with other pacifists, nonviolent resisters, and Christian anarchists, have endured continual hardship in working to eradicate injustices perpetrated by war and violence.

At the time of the First World War, for example, as a way not only of resisting war, but also of demonstrating "a service of love," the Society of Friends in the U.S., with encouragement from English Friends, initiated a service arm of the Society, the American Friends Service Committee. That organization, which maintains regional offices throughout the country, has trained thousands of people for work among refugees around the world and for nonviolent campaigns at home—for civil rights and nuclear disarmament, as well as against the Vietnam and Iraq wars and arms shipments to Central America.

The Mennonites, named for Menno Simons (1496-1561), **231** and the Church of the Brethren both trace their origins to

16th-century Anabaptists, who resisted any union between church and state. Originating in Germany and Switzerland respectively, they believed in freedom of conscience and condemned religious persecution of any kind. The writings of Christopher Sauer, a radical pietist and uncompromising pacifist, influenced both groups in early Pennsylvania, where they joined with their Quaker neighbors in supporting a beneficent government. Sauer, who spoke of soldiers as "military slaves," said that true followers of Jesus could not kill and that participation in war was contrary to the gospel.

At the time of the American Revolution, Mennonites, Brethren, and Quakers composed a significant percentage of the population in the colonies, with the latter group numbering about 50,000 among a total population of 1.6 million. They were responsible for establishing friendly relationships with Native Americans, and later, for making Pennsylvania the first state to abolish slavery. In the 19th century, they provided much of the leadership for the abolitionist movement.

Among the peace churches, their colleges, service committees, and publishing houses are especially important in maintaining and expanding their influence in the wider community. For the Quakers, they include Swarthmore College and Haverford College, in Pennsylvania, and Earlham College, in Indiana; the main office, in Philadelphia, of the American Friends Service Committee, which received the Nobel Prize for Peace in 1947; and the office of Friends Committee on National Legislation, in Washington, D.C. For the Mennonites, they include Eastern Mennonite University, in Virginia; Goshen College, in Indiana; and Bethel College, in Kansas. For the Church of the Brethren, they include McPherson College, in Kansas, and Manchester College, in Indiana. Many peace and justice organizations that eventually became independent of these churches also owe much to their inspiration and guidance. Larger Christian denominations particularly, have much to learn from the peace churches regarding moral issues relating to justice and peace. The following statement by a 232 member of the Church of the Brethren about 18th-century Lutherans, Calvinists, and Catholics remains true today: "What is still more horrible, they go publicly to war, and slaughter one another by the thousands."

In rejecting war, even in revolutionary struggle, the peace churches run risks today similar to those they ran three centuries ago, when they were imprisoned and beaten, their homes seized or burned for their refusal to take up arms against the British. Recognizing "that of God in every person" and "proceeding as the way opens," Quakers choose nonviolence, not because it guarantees results, but because they must, as Margaret Hope Bacon has said. Along that way lies suffering, even death. But only through peaceful means, they argue, does anyone achieve a peaceful end. And even for many who cannot accept the discipline of that life, the historic peace churches—by their witness and experience—remain central to any sustained effort "to construct peace." In their sustained effort to build "the peaceable kingdom" by resolving conflict and initiating social change without killing, they claim particular authority in building nonviolent alternatives to the violence of the status quo.

About Quakers, Mennonites, Church of the Brethren

Bacon, Margaret Hope. *The Quiet Rebels: The Story of the Quakers in America*. Philadelphia: New Society Publishers, 1985.

Brock, Peter. *Pacifism in the U.S. from the Colonial Era to the First World War*. Princeton, N.J.: Princeton University Press, 1968.

Brown, Dale W. *Brethren and Pacifism*. Elgin, Ill.: Brethren Press, 1970.

Keim, Albert N. and Grant M. Stoltzfus. *The Politics of Conscience: The Historic Peace Churches and America at War, 1917-1955*. Scottsdale, Penn.: Herald Press, 1988.

John, H. *What Would You Do? A Serious Answer to a Standard Question*. Scottsdale, Penn.: Herald Press, 1983.

Index

234